# The Joys of Homemaking

## By Daryl V. Hoole

Published by Deseret Book Company
Salt Lake City, Utah
1980

Lithographed by

DESERET PRESS

in the United States of America

*Dedicated to our daughters*
*Jean, Diane, Elaine,*
*Becky, and Nancy*
*and to the three daughters-in-law*
*we hope to have someday*

# Acknowledgments

I am grateful to my husband, Hank, for his enthusiastic support of this and all my other projects and activities in helping other homemakers. I deeply appreciate the excellent manner in which he presides over our home and fulfills his responsibilities as husband, father, and provider.

I'm thankful to my parents, Donovan and Ada Van Dam, who built within me helpful habits and first caused me to see the value of an orderly way of life.

I am indebted to the thousands of women who have given me countless opportunities to learn and grow through sharing and who have contributed a wealth of ideas and information.

# Contents

# 1

## *Bloom Where You're Planted*

*"The most important work
you will ever do
will be within the walls
of your own home."*
*—President Harold B. Lee*

requently women lament to me, "Oh, my house is
in such a mess, and I've no idea where to start in
order to come out of the chaos." Others confess that
the thought of making lists and planning in advance is
completely baffling to them. Still others complain that they
are always behind with their work; and there are mothers
who confide that organizing several children into a team of
cooperative, productive helpers is almost impossible.

During the past few years, whenever the mail, the telephone, or a personal visit has brought a plea for help from
a discouraged woman about a seemingly elementary
household task, I can better understand her plight. Let me
tell you why.

One spring our family undertook a complete redevel-
opment program of our yard. Because neither my husband
nor I has the artistic vision or botanical know-how to
effectively landscape a yard, we engaged the services of a
competent landscape architect. Much to our dismay, not
only did he have to tell us what to plant and where to put
it, but we also needed his detailed advice and complete
instructions on how deep, how far apart, how often to
water, which limb to prune, and so forth, about every piece
of greenery we stuck in the ground.

I've thought about this humbling experience a great
deal. We all have talents and abilities, but we don't all have
the same ones. This is the way our Father in heaven has
allowed us to develop so that we might serve one another
and have opportunity for growth. If we were all lawyers,
who would remove the diseased appendix? If we were all

teachers, who would build the houses? Sometimes we give service and at other times we receive it. In some ways we're teachers and in other ways we are learners or students.

It's important to be worthy of the gifts we have by sharing them generously and helping others to acquire them, if they so desire. Furthermore, we should be humble enough to acknowledge where we are lacking and seek out those who can strengthen and help us. Today, it just takes a stroll through our yard to remind me of all that I don't know and to make me grateful to my Father in heaven for the abilities of others who have helped me and for any gifts I have that might be shared.

In addition to feeling gratitude, I feel excited as new awareness develops. Now my husband and I know something about gardening! We can do a few things without being told; we can find answers to a growing number of our own questions; we have learned many important things about trees, shrubs, and flowers and how to care for them.

In like manner, women who feel perplexed and overwhelmed by household and family cares and responsibilities can also learn how to handle them. This requires a great deal of determination and self-discipline, but step by step it can be done.

We cannot all become experts in every field, but each of us can learn to cope adequately with the responsibilities we have taken upon ourselves. Any woman who has elected to be married and have a family is thereby committed to being an *effective wife, mother, and homemaker*. She owes this to herself, to her family, and to her Father in heaven. These are basic requirements; any other talents are a bonus.

Ever since Eve, I suppose, women have faced the challenges of home and family. In today's world, some of these challenges have become intensified and there are frequently new ones with which to cope.

Perhaps the most significant and threatening of all

challenges to women today are new ideologies. From time to time the mass media taunt us with the "trapped housewife" dilemma. They quote people who claim that if all a woman is is somebody's wife and somebody's mother, then she must be a nobody. It has been said that women are even lower than servants: at least servants are salaried and have regular time off from work. Thus they try to convince us that modern woman is wasting her talents and education in suburbia. Free abortion, so-called foolproof contraceptives, and day-care centers for children are lauded as the answers to women's problems and promise to be the means of their liberation. Some persons of letters and learning denounce marriage and declare that in another generation there will be no need for the unit of society known as the family.

I am grateful that because of my knowledge of the gospel of Jesus Christ, I know who I am and what my mission here on earth is. The diabolical propaganda being circulated only serves to make me more dedicated to my family. I know that I am a wife, mother, and homemaker by divine appointment. I love my work and responsibilities as such; for me, there is nothing more exciting, challenging, satisfying, fulfilling, or worthwhile that I could be doing. I have a wonderful husband; our marriage is a happy, harmonious one; and we are working to make it last forever. Together we are building and influencing the lives of our eight young children. *What greater joy could there be?* All my activities as a mother and homemaker are designed to bear fruit that will hopefully endure for eternity. President David O. McKay said, "I see heaven as the projection of the ideal home into eternity." Not every career can make such a promise.

In a gift shop near our home, a little plaque caught my eye. It read: *BLOOM WHERE YOU'RE PLANTED.* This is just a fun, new way of saying, "Magnify your calling."

It's the prayer of every good Latter-day Saint woman

that her husband will honor his priesthood and magnify his calling as patriarch of the family as well as magnify any position to which he may be called in the Church. It is just as important that we women magnify our callings—bloom where we're planted—as wives, mothers, homemakers, and church workers. It is the intent of this book to help bring this about because I feel it so keenly.

Since teaching my first homemaking class for Brigham Young University Continuing Education in 1960 and subsequently having published my first book, *The Art of Homemaking*, two years later, I have enjoyed a multitude of experiences with homemakers and their challenges. This great exposure has caused me to become aware of many problems and some solutions; dozens of ideas for improving home and family have come to my attention; a number of helpful stories and first-hand experiences have been shared with me.

I have felt a growing impression to make all this available to women on a far broader basis than just through my classes; thus, this book has been written as a supplement or sequel to *The Art of Homemaking*. It also treats the basics: the organization of space and time and the effective handling of children. These ideas represent a never-ending interest to countless women. The many women who return time after time to classes to hear these fundamental principles will hopefully like this approach. Also, my contacts over these years have given me additional insight into what women really need—what helps them most. I have earnestly endeavored to include these ideas in this book.

Some old ideas that have proven extremely valuable have been developed to a greater extent than they were in *The Art of Homemaking*. For instance, whereas that book described toy bags and treasure chests in paragraphs, this book will use several pages to give further application and explanation of them. I have learned that knowing how to file and then find things is important for many women. Thus, the page or so about filing that was found in the previous book has grown into a detailed illustrated explanation in this volume. And the many women who are ready to move on to new ideas, philosophies, stories, and concepts will also be able to glean helps from these pages.

However, books such as mine are not necessarily meant for every homemaker. Some women are so proficient in the home that they don't need help any more than Betty Crocker needs a cooking course. On the other hand, the fact that they are so very qualified often makes home and family their favorite subject, and they love reading material on these subjects.

Some women don't want to learn anything about homemaking. Once while I was lecturing on this subject, a woman happened to come into my class by mistake—she had really intended to listen to someone else who was teaching that hour. When she sat down, there was a faint gasp throughout the group, as her neighbors saw her there. I later learned that she was well known for her housekeeping—or rather, she was well known for her lack of housekeeping. Well, she remained the entire hour. A few days later one of her neighbors asked her what she had thought about the class. She replied, "Daryl Hoole's lecture didn't do a thing for me." Then, after some hesitation, she added, "Well, after the class I did clean out my purse."

There are many women in between the extremes of those who don't need additional help or those who don't want it. Perhaps they are the ones who just want their "clocks rewound." Someone once said, "Inspiration doesn't last, but then, neither does a bath." Maybe they're looking for some new ideas to give fuel to their self-starters.

Other women are searching for new techniques or improved skills. It's amazing how unprepared some brides are as they enter marriage. One newlywed called her mother one day and said, "I've just made a cake and doubled the recipe. But I don't know how to bake it, because my oven won't go to 700 degrees." (I told that story to a group of teenage girls once and no one laughed!)

Some women need motivation and discipline. One day after one of my lectures, a woman approached me and declared, "I'm the world's worst housekeeper." I often hear such comments and never quite know how to respond, so I began by probing a little. I inquired if perhaps she had a health problem, to which she assured me that she was "as strong as a horse." Then I asked if she had several small children who required care all the time. No, that wasn't a problem; her youngest child was four. She also assured me she had a fairly nice, convenient home, and her husband was not a busy doctor or farmer nor did he work the swing shift. Finally she confessed the problem: "I'm just lazy."

Regardless of the situation or problem, the fortunate woman, the one who is on the road toward ultimate success, is the one who is determined to master herself and gain the necessary skills. One distraught mother with stacks of clothing to be washed, much clutter throughout her house, children fussing, and the sink piled with dishes finally hung her Phi Beta Kappa key over the kitchen sink and declared to herself, "If I was smart enough to get that, I should be able to accomplish this!"

In overcoming problems and mastering new skills, it's important to attempt it only one step at a time. If one tries to go in all directions at once, she'll arrive nowhere. Remember, perfection is a process, not an event.

A friend whom I'll call Pamela really made this work in her life. She attended a class I taught that was comprised of university students' wives. I barely noticed her at the time, but a few weeks later as I was teaching a class in another part of the city, there she was again. Then she appeared once more in another class the next month. As we became acquainted, I learned her story.

Pamela's mother had passed away when Pamela was a very young girl, and as a result she had never been taught homemaking skills—not even good habits about bed-making and picking up after herself—and she had never been involved in a happy, normal family situation, so she didn't know how such a situation functions. Thus, when she married and then had a family, she felt completely at a loss. She had a college degree and was knowledgeable about many things—but not about homemaking. Her husband was getting an advanced degree from the university, and she felt that she needed to be professional in her field too, which was now homemaking. She said she was getting a Ph.D. all right, but for the wrong thing. Hers was for "piling it higher and deeper."

Pamela was determined to do something about it, one step at a time. Getting up earlier in the morning was step number one, she decided. She confessed that she had been in the habit of escaping reality and avoiding the responsibilities of the day by staying in bed most of the morning. She wouldn't get up until the cries of her children and cold cereal scattered from wall to wall forced her to do so. She knew it was wrong to sleep so late, but it required all of her thought, concentration, determination, and will power to conquer the problem. All day long she'd have to say to herself, over and over again, "Pam, tomorrow you'll get up on time." At first she had to literally force herself out of bed, but after a few weeks the day came when it wasn't such an effort any more.

Then she took my class again and decided that the next step was to learn to follow up after herself and put away whatever she had used. Never in her life had anyone taught her to be neat and orderly. It wasn't the children or her husband who were the problems—it was mommy herself. Once again, learning to put things away took all of her thought, concentration, determination, and will power. Throughout the day she'd go through the mental process of saying to herself, "I'm taking off my coat now and I must hang it in this closet....I've used the car keys and I must return them to my purse and then put my purse on this shelf....I've finished reading the book, and I must put it back in the bookcase."

Needless to say, there wasn't much time in her life for a creative or spiritual thought until she had mastered her problem. But she did master it after awhile, and she found much to her delight that when a good habit replaced a bad one, a whole new dimension of freedom opened up in her life.

Step number three was to do the dishes after each meal. It had been her habit to let soiled dishes accumulate for several days—until there were no clean ones to eat from. To overcome this fault, she'd say to herself, "Pam, you cannot leave the kitchen until you've done the dishes." She made it work!

Step by step Pam progressed until she called on me at our home one day. She was thrilled because her husband had just received his doctorate and had secured a fine position teaching college. But, she added, "It's what has happened to me that pleases us the most. It's really my commencement. I'm prepared to leave our little apartment and move into a house and make it a home. I know how to be a good homemaker and mother, and I have the habits and abilities to do so."

Think what an accomplishment this is! Pamela had completely realigned her habits and life-style. That's a literal operation bootstrap. She did not have the innate ability to be a good homemaker, so she didn't have anything to draw from. But she put the ability into herself and then she could get it out. Pamela's story can be proof to anyone that it can be done. Changing and improving, doing away with poor habits and making better ones, is one of life's most basic challenges. The following words, by an unknown author, illustrate this:

I am your constant companion. I am your greatest helper—or your heaviest burden. I will push you onward or drag you down to failure. I am completely at your command. Half the tasks you do you might just as well turn over to me and I will be able to do them quickly and correctly.

I am easily managed. You must merely be firm with me. Show me exactly how you want something done, and after a few lessons, I will do it automatically.

I am the servant of all great men—and, alas, of all failures as well. Those who are great, I have made great. Those who are failures, I have made failures.

I am not a machine, but I work with all the precision of a machine, plus the intelligence of a man. You may run me for profit or run me for ruin. It makes no difference to me.

Take me, train me, be firm with me, and I will put the world at your feet. Be easy with me and I will destroy you.

Who am I? I am HABIT.

We can do much for ourselves through gaining self-mastery, or self-ownership, as I like to call it. But as noble as our own efforts may be, we can progress only to a point through them. There is a higher law by which we must live if we are to fully overcome ourselves.

In order to reach for perfection, we need the blessings, strengths, and gifts that come from our Father in heaven. These can be ours if we prepare ourselves spiritually and get on our knees and talk to our Heavenly Father about them. The most inspiring part of this is to realize that the closer we come to the Lord through understanding and knowing him and communicating with him, the greater will be our motivation and ability to gain victory over ourselves. Only then can we truly attain our goal of being prepared for celestial living.

If our long-range goal is exaltation as a family in the celestial kingdom, our intermediate goal must be to have a happy, loving family now. The only way to have our home in heaven someday is to have some heaven in our home here on earth. Then it follows that our immediate goal is to live the laws of righteousness through establishing a house of order, both physically and spiritually.

In the 1973-74 *Family Home Evening Manual,* President Harold B. Lee gave this definition of the ideal home:

> The primary function of a Latter-day Saint home is to ensure that every family member works to create the climate and condition in which all can grow toward perfection. For the parents, this requires a dedication of time and energy far beyond the mere providing of their children's physical needs. For the children, this means controlling the natural tendency toward selfishness.
>
> Do you spend as much time making your family and home successful as you do in pursuing social and professional success? Are you devoting your best creative energy to the most important unit in society—the family; or is your relationship with your family merely a routine, unrewarding part of your life?
>
> Parents and children must be willing to put family responsibilities first in order to achieve family exaltation.

A capable, lovely homemaker and mother usually (1) has had the good fortune of growing up in a fine home where things were orderly and systematic and very pleasant, and where good habits, self-discipline, and a love for people were instilled within her; (2) has learned these things through classes in school; or (3) is naturally talented in domestic arts and human relations.

But what if you feel you weren't taught and you aren't

so talented? Don't despair, and don't use these reasons as an excuse. We can learn a good lesson about excuses from the parable of the talents, as found in Matthew. There we are told of three servants who received talents—five, two, and one, respectively. Upon their master's return, each one rendered account of his stewardship. The first two had doubled their talents, or capital, and each reported so in sixteen words. Of their work, the master said, "Well done, thou good and faithful servant." The third servant had accomplished absolutely nothing, but he took forty-three words to report, almost three times as many words as the others used.

There you have it. The less you do, the more you have to explain. So forget about excuses. They are meaningless. You can learn to be a good homemaker if you haven't already done so. Truly you can!

It does require much effort. Remember the story of the two men who had not seen each other since their school days and who happened to meet again. One confessed to the other, "I got married because I was tired of going to the laundromat, eating in restaurants, and wearing socks with holes in them." "That's funny," the other replied. "I just got divorced for the same reasons."

Some people take a negative viewpoint and feel that housework is something a woman does that no one notices unless she leaves it undone. Fortunately, that isn't the case. Many people do appreciate a lovely cared-for home and admire the woman who keeps it that way. One woman explained her plan of action. She said, "If it moves, I feed it. If it doesn't, I dust it."

Many young brides begin their marriages with just the right touch for making their husbands happy and their houses shine. For others, it's more of a gradual process as they learn and improve each year. There are also a number of very commendable women who make a sudden, drastic, and dramatic improvement in their homemaking. Almost overnight, it seems, they abandon poor habits, make good new ones, and become wonderful homemakers. I'll never forget the grateful husband whose wife made an abrupt about-face in her homemaking efforts. "After eleven years of marriage," he said, "my wife has at last become the woman I thought I married."

To many, homemaking is still an uphill climb. Not every woman with a house to keep has the necessary know-how for doing it well. Some fall short in domestic prowess. A magazine writer, interviewing a young woman, asked, "Tell me, do you feel that your work as a homemaker is beneath you?" "Oh, no," was the response, "I feel it's beyond me!" The following chapters have been written so that, hopefully, homemaking will never be either beneath or beyond you.

"Organize yourselves; prepare every needful thing; and establish a house, even a house of prayer, a house of fasting, a house of faith, a house of learning, a house of glory, a house of order, a house of God." (Doctrine and Covenants 88:119.)

# 2
## Put It All Together, It Spells "Mother"

*A wise woman
makes her home
her business.*

I left my secretarial position early in 1958 to prepare for the arrival of our first baby. As I was closing up my desk for the last time to become a full-time home-maker, it suddenly occurred to me that there was a definite correlation between successful office procedures and good homemaking. A whole new concept in living opened up before me.

Aside from the efficiency techniques that can help both businesses and homes, I came to realize as a young home-maker that an hour or so a day at the typewriter in our home, handling correspondence, keeping our home filing system current, and working on family histories, scrap-books, and other paper projects, kept me in touch with my profession as a secretary. I felt professional at home too, and as a result I never missed the office. I discovered there were many incentives and compensations associated with working for myself, so to speak. I liked being my own boss. Time was mine to use as I saw it best. All my "office" duties had significance to me and our family.

My neighbor across the street, a dietician by training, added her professional touches to family mealtimes. I learned from her, and again I felt a bit more specialized as a homemaker.

While driving through a housing development for mar-ried university students, I was charmed by artwork, as only four- and five-year-olds can create it, greeting me from the windowpanes of one apartment. I knew the mother there—a former kindergarten teacher. The school bell didn't lure her anymore; she was teaching at home. Her students

were her very own children. What an incentive toward ap-
plying all the techniques and ideas of effective professional
teaching!

I thought of another friend who sang beautifully and
was an accomplished musician. How enriched her children's lives were through her talents!

I visited the home of a young bride who had majored
in interior design. She had never actually held a job in her
chosen field, but she was using her training well in her own
home. I was inspired by what I saw, and I determined to
engage in a little private study of interior design for the
benefit of our home.

I thought of others: nurses, beauticians, sociologists—
all using their professional training to enhance their roles
as wives, mothers, and homemakers.

In this age of specialization and sophisticated training,
it is exciting to see how much of it can apply in the home.
In fact, as someone said, "Put it all together, it spells
'Mother.'"

Asked by the woman recorder to state her
"occupation," Emily hesitated, uncertain how to
classify herself.

"What I mean," explained the recorder, "is—do
you have a job or are you just a..."

"Of course I have a job," snapped Emily. "I'm
a mother!"

Then the recorder smiled indulgently. She
wrote: "Occupation: housewife."

"Oh, no," protested Emily. "I'd rather be listed
as a mother."

"We don't list mother as an occupation. Housewife covers it," said the recorder.

I forgot all about her story until one day I found
myself in the same situation. The clerk was obviously a career woman, poised, efficient, and
possessed of a high-sounding title like "Official

Interrogator" or "Town Registrar."

"And what is your occupation?" she probed.

What made me say it, I do not know. The words simply popped out. "I'm a research associate in the field of Child Development and Human Relations."

The clerk paused, ballpoint pen frozen in mid-air, and looked up as though she had not heard right. I repeated the title slowly, emphasizing the most significant words.

"Might I ask," said the clerk with new interest, "just what you do in your field?"

Coolly, without any trace of fluster in my voice, I heard myself reply, "I have a continuing program of research (what mother doesn't?) in the laboratory and in the field (normally I would have said 'indoors and out'). I'm working for my masters (the whole darned family!) and already have four credits (four daughters). Of course, the job is one of the most demanding, work-a-14-hour day (24 hours is more like it). But the job is more challenging than most run-of-the-mill careers and the rewards are in satisfaction rather than 'just money.'"

There was an increasing note of respect in the clerk's voice as she completed the form, stood up, and personally ushered me to the door.

As I drove into our driveway, buoyed up by my glamorous new career, I was greeted by my "lab assistants"—ages 13, 7, and 3. And upstairs, I could hear our new experimental model (6 months) in the child development program testing out a new vocal pattern.

I felt triumphant. I had scored a beat on bureaucracy. And I had gone down on the official records as someone more distinguished and indispensable to mankind than "just another..."

Home. What a glorious career! Especially when

there's a new title on the door.
    —Author Unknown

The more intelligent, talented, capable, creative, and educated a woman is, the richer can be her life and the lives of those in her family. In this way she's a homemaker, not just a housewife. And she teaches her children, instead of merely tends them.

Even the woman who, due to extraordinary circumstances, finds it necessary to be employed outside the home can bless her family through her training and experience. She must exert special effort and be alert to all possibilities to do this, but it can be done.

One poet has written:

*ON NEST BUILDING*

*Mud is not bad for nest building.*
*Mud and sticks*
*And a fallen feather or two will do,*
*And require no reaching.*
*I could rest there, with my tiny ones,*
*Sound for the season, at least.*

*But—*
*If I may fly awhile—*
*If I may cut through a sunset going out*
*And a rainbow coming back,*
*Color upon color sealed in my eyes—*
*If I may have the unboundaried skies*
*For my study,*
*Clouds, cities, rivers, for my rooms—*
*If I may search the centuries*
*For melody and meaning—*
*If I may try for the sun—*

*I shall come back*
*Bearing such beauties*
*Gleaned from God's and man's very best,*
*I shall come filled.*

*And then—*
*Oh, the nest that I can build!*

    *—Carol Lynn Pearson*

A home holds all the areas of achievement that can be found in any field. It isn't necessary to venture into the business world for excitement and challenges. A wise woman makes her home her business.

# 3
## Start Here!

*"We shape our houses,*
*then our houses shape us."*
—Sir Winston Churchill

I once heard an eminent scientist say, "It takes intelligence to create order." That being the case, you can figure out for yourself what it takes to make a mess!

There are a number of good reasons for keeping an orderly home: what it does for the appearance of the house, what it does for the progress within the home (no need to elaborate on the advantages of quickly locating both socks, finding a pair of scissors or a sharpened pencil, etc.), and the special things it does for the family.

When a home reflects tender, loving care, everyone benefits. Young children grow up with good habits; self-discipline is built in. Children who see their parents do their best and excel in their work are usually motivated to do likewise. (By the same token, parents who are slothful and lazy often produce children who are inclined to follow suit.) An orderly home can encourage creativity: supplies are easily located, work surfaces and areas are available, and a general feeling of progress and excellence permeates the household.

There were many problems at the home of Mr. and Mrs. Blank. The husband's paycheck was far from adequate. As a result, bills were stacked high and financial problems plagued them from all sides. The children were out of control and caused problems wherever they went. Mrs. Blank felt about five years behind in her housework. She was so depressed that she had developed a serious case of inertia. The situation worsened with each day.

At the very bleakest point, a neighbor happened to give Mrs. Blank a bouquet of fresh flowers. It had been a long time since she had held fresh flowers in her hands, so she took a minute to admire them. Then she went into the house and found a little container for them and put them on the kitchen table. But the table was so littered that the flowers were completely lost there, so she cleared the table off. She then noticed how worn and bare the tabletop was, so she found a cloth to cover it and then put the flowers back. They really did look charming, she thought, as she stood back to look at them—but the effect was quickly spoiled by the neglect in the rest of the room. So she tidied that room up, which led to the next room, and the next one, until the whole house was in order. Then she herself felt out of place in her appearance, so she put on some fresh clothes and brushed her hair.

At this point something interesting happened. Mrs. Blank felt a surge of ambition go through her. (It's not what you've done that makes you tired; it's what you haven't done that's so exhausting. A day's work completed is really quite exhilarating. It's when you are halfway through the work and see that you are not going to make it that fatigue sets in.) Well, with this newfound energy, Mrs. Blank fussed over dinner that night. She seasoned the vegetables and meat especially well, managed to make some tasty gravy, and baked a pudding. As the children came home from school, instead of screaming and tearing through the house as they usually did, they exclaimed, "Mom, what's happened? Who's coming? What can we do to help?" And they were actually cooperative and pleasant.

Later Mr. Blank arrived home. But instead of greeting his family with his usual gripes and complaints, he was complimentary and congenial. His mood matched the atmosphere. His mood had always matched the atmosphere—it's just that this day the atmosphere had changed.

The family sat around the table enjoying the tastiest meal they could ever remember, with the flowers as the centerpiece. While they were eating, the landlord came to

serve an eviction notice because they were so far behind
in their rent payments. But as he entered the room and
looked around, he changed his mind and said, "Oh, I see
things are improving. I'll give you another month to meet
the payment." And things did improve, because when the
mother cared and tried, the husband and children did too.

Yes, much can be said about what an orderly home
does for the family, but even more can be said about what
it can do for the homemaker herself. To me, our home is
my little world. All I see for many hours a day are the four
walls there, so I've decided to make my world just the way
I want it. Even though the big world outside may be full
of problems, at least my world inside my home can be
peaceful, pleasant, and progressive. I've learned that pretty
colors in paint don't cost any more than ugly colors do, so
why not have colors I enjoy?

Homey touches—evidence of creativity here and there
—help make me glad to be there. Good taste knows no
price tag. Interesting, well-arranged wall groupings; bright
floral arrangements; lush plants; skillfully refinished pieces
of furniture; colorful toss pillows; gay curtains; little things
displayed that tell stories about the people who live there—
all mean a lot to me.

Unless it's charming, I want it out of sight. I'm offended
by window sills lined with spray cans, cartons, and bottles,
or mantels and dresser tops cluttered with junk. The
kitchen counter is not an annex to the cupboard at our
house, with jam and peanut butter containers, cracker
boxes, and other assorted supplies lining it. I like it free
from all such things except for a cookie jar, a bowl of fruit,
some potted plants at the window, and perhaps a small
appliance or so. When I'm cooking, there's plenty of space
to set out twelve dozen cookies (with our big family, that's
how many we bake at a time!), roll out pie crust or pizza,
arrange salads, or bake bread. And between projects, the
kitchen can be in complete order.

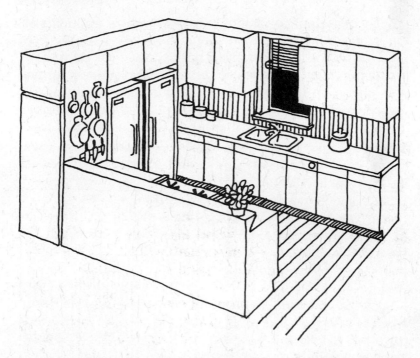

Some kitchens never really look "done." They are just a constant round of clutter of many things that have no place. (One of my favorite things about a dishwasher is that it's such a good hiding place for the glasses and dishes that inevitably accumulate.) To me, a shining, orderly kitchen does wonders for my attitude, ambition, efficiency, and nerves.

Of course, many kitchens are small and congested and have no dishwashers or other conveniences. The home-maker who manages well under such conditions is really to be admired! If things have to be stacked, at least they can be stacked neatly. Sometimes storing things away or throwing some things away helps alleviate the problem. While preparing a meal or baking, the homemaker can have handy a sink or pan filled with hot, sudsy water to keep the dishwashing current. Small kitchens *can* be neat, and inconvenient conditions *can* be improved upon. It's all up to the homemaker.

Not only is it important to have a place for everything in the home and to have everything in its place, but it matters also a lot how you do it. Putting things away neatly conserves a lot of space, but best of all it has an almost magical effect on the homemaker. If a closet looks well-

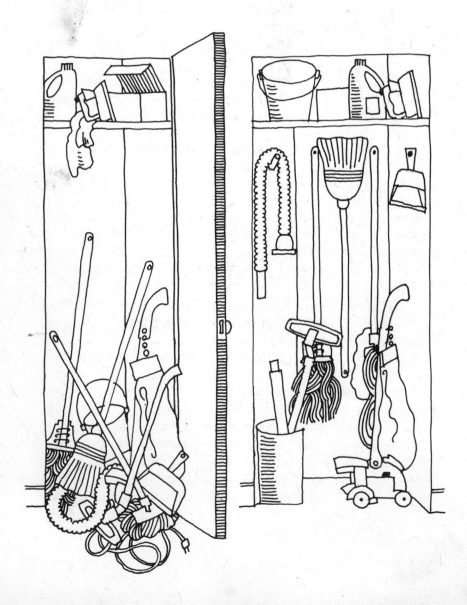

arranged and organized, it says, "Mrs. Homemaker, you are doing well," and you fairly fly to the next task. Conversely, if you open a close door and it appears that a bomb just went off in there, you feel like a complete drudge and have to drag yourself to the next job.

The better one does, the better she can continue to do. Women learn to generate their own energy. Success begets success; on the other hand, failure begets failure. Which pattern is in effect in your home? If it's the latter one, here's how to make the breakthrough with regard to closets:

1. Go see some well-arranged closets and cupboards in someone's home or look up some in homemaking magazines or books. Close your eyes and visualize your own closet in tip-top shape.

2. Allow yourself to take a step backward so you can go several steps forward. In other words, you might have to let a few things go while you organize your closets and cupboards. Simplify the meals and let the vacuuming and dusting wait for a few days. One doesn't get too far behind in the cleaning in a couple of days' time—one swipe and the dirt is gone. Do keep up the washing, however. If you don't, it will continue to mount and disrupt the entire household.

3. Tackle only one closet or cupboard at a time. One that is put in good order is worth six that are unloaded in the middle of the room.

4. Procure and use large containers for things to give away, throw away, and store away.

5. Go to work! You'll gain more than an improved storage area; there will be a better you.

The information in this chapter easily applies to the average home with the normal challenges of establishing and maintaining order. But let's discuss, for a minute, houses that are inhabited by litterbugs, or so it seems, and where clutter seems as permanent as the furniture.

Often women complain that for one reason or another, they feel hopelessly behind in their housework or they are up to their knees, so to speak, in clutter, and they don't know where to start coming out of the mess. It seems that when things get this bad, attempting to pick up is almost a hopeless task. It's like digging in a sandhill: when one shovelful is removed, two others slide in its place.

A woman called me on the phone one day and, in a voice choked with sobs, said, "As my husband left for work this morning he said he had had it with the clutter and mess around here. He declared that if it were still like this when he got home this evening, he was packing up and leaving." She pleaded for help.

A drastic solution to such a desperate situation can be the leaf-bag approach: making rounds of the house and literally scooping all the clutter into large plastic bags. Then either give away or dispose of the bags (the disorganized contents weren't really serving the family anyway in their confused state) or take them to the garage or some similar place to be sorted, one at a time. In either event, the house is freed from the mess and housekeeping can move forward. In extreme cases, women have reported that this clean-sweep approach is the only way they've been able to start functioning in their housework.

Now, on with some suggestions for an orderly home.

1. *Always leave the house orderly before retiring at night.*

Toys, projects, and clothing should be put away, with each family member responsible for his own things as soon as he is old enough. The kitchen should also be cleared from snacks and meals. This has a calming effect on me—I feel thoroughly relaxed—and the next morning I'm ahead before I've even opened my eyes. Some women begin each day two hours behind! Enjoy the numerous advantages of working ahead of yourself, rather than behind yourself.

2. *Lay a foundation early and well.*

I like to compare managing a home to building a house, with a foundation, a cornerstone, and a structure. The cornerstone is to take care of me. I like to get up and dressed first thing in the morning. I've learned that the sooner I'm dressed, the more successful is my day! I can work twice as fast in proper clothing, I feel more like doing the part if I look the part, and family members respect me more when I'm groomed. (One who looks like a doormat should expect to be walked over!) Take the necessary time to keep up your personal appearance.

Laying the foundation means doing the basic, routine morning work—picking things up, wiping things off. It's just a quick skim through the house, making beds, tidying up, clearing tables, running the dishwasher and washer/dryer, sweeping floors, taking care of children. The foundation should be laid by about ten o'clock each morning, give or take a little. Of course, if there is a new baby or several small children, it will require considerably longer until they learn to feed and dress themselves, make their own beds, and help with the daily routine.

Once the foundation is laid, you may choose how to build that day. You may do such things as (a) clean house, (b) guide and teach children, (c) cook or bake, (d) sew or mend, (e) shop or run errands, (f) garden or decorate, (g) attend meetings or keep appointments, (h) study or read, (i) engage in special projects or other activities.

Generally speaking, you'll be amazed at how high you can build. Of course, you won't be able to build all day long. There will be more routine duties, such as preparing meals and changing diapers; however, they can be building experiences too, depending upon your attitude, and a great deal of progress can still be made.

One difficulty is that some women never get to the point of building. It takes them all day long to get the routine work done. They never seem to get past the point of sweeping up the crumbs, doing the dishes, or making the beds. They need lots of help in getting organized and getting their children to help them. Other women have difficulty laying a foundation of routine work because they are too thorough too soon. They can't just wipe off a fingerprint—they must wash the entire wall. They can't just brush up a few crumbs or ravelings—they must vacuum the entire carpet.

Some women also attempt to build without ever laying the foundation. They work backwards, putting second things first. Of course, things just crumble and tumble all about them as a result. A classic example of this concerns a woman who was making her bed one morning about 7:30 when she noticed a clothes closet nearby that needed straightening. So she abandoned the bed halfway through making it and started working on the closet. She became engrossed with that project, reading, sorting, rearranging things, and it consumed her entire day. Late that afternoon her husband returned hom to find neglected children, breakfast dishes still on the table, a partially made bed, and his wife (still in her bathrobe) in the closet. He scolded her for never getting anything done, and she burst into tears and told him how hard she had worked—in the clothes closet. If she had just turned the day around and worked on the closet after the routine work had been completed, it would have been a super day for her.

A good home manager first of all keeps order, lays the foundation, and then builds. No matter how the windows might sparkle or the floors might shine, your efforts won't be noticed or appreciated if the table isn't cleared or if the living room is cluttered.

The First Presidency has issued a statement emphasizing the importance of keeping our homes in order:

> We earnestly call upon members of the Church
> everywhere to clean up and beautify their homes,
> surroundings, farms and places of business.

Our homes and building are the showcases of what we believe. They should be attractive and give every indication of cleanliness, orderliness, and self-esteem. (Message dated September 1974.)

3. *Practice the picking-up process.*

Once the foundation is laid, maintain it during the day. Don't let things fall apart. With convenient pockets in your clothes, make it a habit to keep things picked up as you walk through your home and yard. I'll always remember a lovely homemaker whom we visited one afternoon. Just as we were leaving she said to her children, "Daddy will be home from work soon. Make certain the family room is in order and the rest of the house is neat so he will know we've done our work too."

4. *Establish some ground rules.*

On the premise that an ounce of prevention is worth many pounds of cure, a few rules can be very helpful. Children like rules. It's like lines on the freeway to a motorist: it's confusing and frightening to drive without them but reassuring to drive with them. Some rules might be:

a. No eating on foot. It's not necessary or permissible to scatter crumbs and sticky spots throughout the house.

b. He who snacks also clears up.

c. No one may leave for school, play, or any other activity until his room is in order.

d. Don't leave the bathroom until it's tidy.

e. Hang up your clothes.

f. Projects are encouraged, but please do them where spills and spatters can easily be wiped up, and then put away supplies when you are through with them. In other words, the Boy Scout philosophy applies: "Leave an area better than you found it."

5. *Be brave enough to throw or give things away.*

Many of us have "pioneer blood" in our veins, so to speak, and find it difficult to throw things away. We have the feeling that we must save almost everything in case we need it sometime. It is true, many things should be kept. But some people save too much. Unless an item should be kept for emergency purposes, or unless it fits into your storage or filing systems, or specifically relates to a facet of your life, you're probably better off without it.

    6. *Store things properly.*

    Items to be kept should be stored in good order. Our home is filled with closets and cupboards, but somehow with all ten of us living here, there isn't enough room in

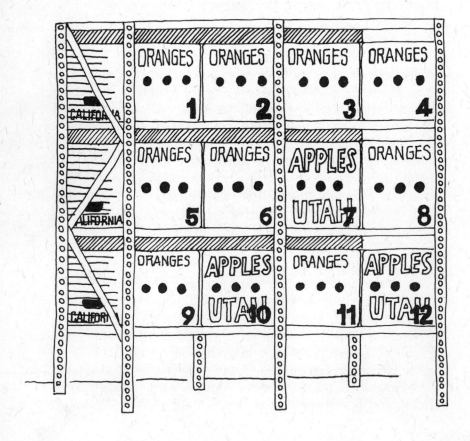

those closets for holiday decorations, clothing the children might wear a year or two hence, and other odds and ends. These items we have placed in covered cardboard fruit boxes along one wall of our garage. The boxes may be labeled as to their contents, or a more workable system might be to number them and use a master sheet—a list of the boxes and their contents—to direct you to a box you might wish to locate. A good storage system saves space, time, and money. It's a must for every house.

7. *Organize toys for fun, not frustration.*

Have you ever heard a mother cry, "We're through buying toys for the children! They become lost or scattered so quickly that it's just a waste of money to buy new ones." Or another mother bemoans the fact that toys keep her house looking like a tickertape parade had just passed by. Still another mother sighs and says, "Every night we have to pick up every toy in the house."

Such feelings are reflected by countless parents—with good reason. As children grow larger, their toys become smaller and come in more and more pieces. In fact, toys can be extremely complex; some building sets, for instance, have hundreds of parts. The question is, how can toys be handled so they don't turn into junk at the bottom of some box or become lost and scattered over the neighborhood or litter the house?

There's also another problem to consider. The boxes toys come in are usually flimsy and soon break down at the corners. Besides, the boxes often contain stuffer or filler, causing them to take up more than their share of space. A workable solution is to prepare individual containers for toys that come in pieces or parts. Drawstring bags of varying sizes and colors made from gay-colored denim and labeled with a marking pen make ideal containers for blocks, Lincoln Logs, guidance toys of all sorts, and similar items. Cans or cartons, such as empty shortening cans with plastic seals or empty ice cream cartons, are

great for puzzle pieces, crayons, and marbles. Smaller containers, such as those for cottage cheese or sour cream,
are just right for storing the parts to games. For example,
all the pieces for one game might be in one container and
those for another game in another container. Then just
stack the game boards with the instructions pasted on their
backs. Bags may be hung on a pegboard or kept in a

drawer, while cans and cartons may be stored on shelves or any similar convenient place.

These containers do conserve space, and they keep toys well organized so the children can play with them for the purpose for which they are intended. Few children have the patience to sort through a box of toys to get together enough little plastic bricks, for example, to build something. If the pieces are not sorted and manageable, they'll just dump the box and make a mess. This system of using individual containers also rotates the toys so the children don't see every toy every day. When a bag is opened after not having been used for several weeks, the toys it contains are almost like new to the children. Best of all, the bags and containers come with a rule. You've probably guessed it: no new bags or containers can be opened until the contents of the last one (or several containers, depending on the toys needed for play) have been picked up. This makes picking up part of the game, instead of mother's having to pick up dozens of toys at the end of the day when the children are tired and she is harried.

Make it a point to give your children special containers for their toys as they receive new toys. Be firm in teaching them to pick up what has been played with before going on to the next project. You'll discover that this bit of care and organization can keep toys and games in good order for years, keep your house free of littered toys, and provide maximum enjoyment for your children.

8. *Make a treasure chest for each child.*

Have you prepared a keepsake box for each of your children? If not, how about considering it? All you need is a large pasteboard box—empty orange or apple boxes with secure tops, obtained from the grocery store, make ideal ones—covered with each child's favorite color and design in stick-on paper. Then name it a treasure chest or whatever you and your child like, and begin the exciting venture of filling it.

A treasure chest might contain a baby book, scrap-
book, heirlooms from grandparents and great-grandpar-
ents, souvenirs and mementoes from trips and special
occasions, and a book of remembrance. Copies of certifi-
cates and papers of significance may be placed in books
and kept in the treasure chest. (The originals should be
kept in a safety deposit box or other secure place if you
don't feel they belong in the treasure chest.) The treasure
chest might also hold a child's last doll or some other cher-
ished toy.

A manila envelope—one for each year of the child's life
—is just the thing for a few selected school papers. If all
school papers are saved, they amount to a big pile of junk;
however, a few choice ones can become treasures over
the years. (Besides, every child needs to develop the self-
discipline to throw some things away.) The manila enve-
lopes might also be just the right place to keep samples of
arts and crafts projects.

A recently widowed lady remarked that she had just
spent two days going through everything in her house looking for her marriage license, which she needed for estate
purposes. One of our children who overheard her statement later commented, "If she had a treasure chest, it
wouldn't have taken her two days to find something important." Everyone does need a specific, safe place for important papers and items of value.

It's a rewarding experience to introduce a child to his
treasure chest. This can be done when he's about three
years old or mature enough to look at a picture without
crumpling it. It's impressive to observe how quickly he
grasps the significance of his treasure chest and becomes
delighted with its contents. Then gradually over the years
it becomes more meaningful to him. Under Mother's wise
guidance, he eventually learns to discern between things
to throw away and treasures to cherish and is able to take
the responsibility of his treasure chest himself. For a really

special Christmas or birthday gift, consider obtaining a box, gathering keepsakes, and making a treasure chest for each one of your children. It does much more than provide the child with a specific place for valuables; it also gives him a deep sense of security, and in order for one to have hopes and dreams for the future, he needs some memories of the past.

9. *Know how to file it and find it again.*

As homemakers who need to keep track of instructions, warranties, patterns; as community leaders who want to find copies of documents and other items pertaining to their responsibilities; as members of the Church who find special stories or thoughts and want to keep them for future talks or lessons, there has to be an answer. Many of us are great collectors of such materials, but few of us can ever find what we need quickly. All too often we spend hours, even days, searching through books and papers for specific things. The solution is an effective home filing system.

The system that does the best job for me is called a *master file system,* patterned after the card catalog at the public library. When you go to the library for a book, you first look up the book's title in the card catalog, where it is listed on various cards according to author, title, and subject. A number then directs you to the proper shelf.

This system also works beautifully on a smaller scale in a home. I have a small master file, or card catalog, in which every item in my filing cabinet is listed on a 4″ x 6″ card. This is done according to title (if there is one), author (if the name is important to me; otherwise I omit that card), and subjects (several of them, if necessary). Then a number leads me to the item in my filing cabinet or other storage areas.

In the filing cabinet itself, items are placed in order numerically. I have about 25 items in each file folder, since that seems to be about right so the folder is neither too thick nor too thin. The first manila folder holds items 1 to 25; the second, 26 to 50; and so forth. In other words, I place items in the filing cabinet in the order in which I get them. In any one folder containing 25 items, there might be 25 different subjects. It's the *master card file* that serves as an index to help me locate a particular one. Even though this system may appear to be involved at first, it makes sense as soon as it is thoroughly understood, and it is simple and fast to use. For supplies you need:

a. A container for your file entries. A pasteboard box works well, if you don't wish to buy a filing cabinet; you may also be able to find an inexpensive second-hand file. Personally, I prefer a legal-size filing cabinet, which is two inches larger than the standard size.

b. Manila folders or more durable plastic folders found in many office supply stores.

c. A small file box for your master file.

d. A supply of 4" x 6" file cards.

e. Some 4" x 6" dividers with alphabetized tabs.

With the aid of detailed instructions and illustrations, let's go through the actual steps of filing an item. Let's say I want to place in my file the following quotation by David O. McKay: "Spirituality is consciousness of victory over self and communion with the infinite."

If this is the first entry in my file, I would place the arabic numeral 1 in the upper righthand corner of the entry. Next, I would make several index cards for the master file, with the subjects under which I might look for this quotation: Spirituality, Self-Discipline, Prayer, etc. I would also make a card for the author, McKay, David O.

I would then place the index cards alphabetically in the master file, and finally I would place the quotation itself in the first file folder and put it in my filing cabinet or whatever container I'm using.

Some of the advantages and bonus features of the master file system are:

a. It simplifies decision making. You can list an item according to the title, author, and subject. You'll find that many items don't have a clearly defined subject; others are a composite of several topics; and some are just generally edifying. This index system eliminates the frustration of categorizing items and then locating them. The system is workable because you can locate things from various angles. For example, I have in my file an excellent article on stewardship that is indexed

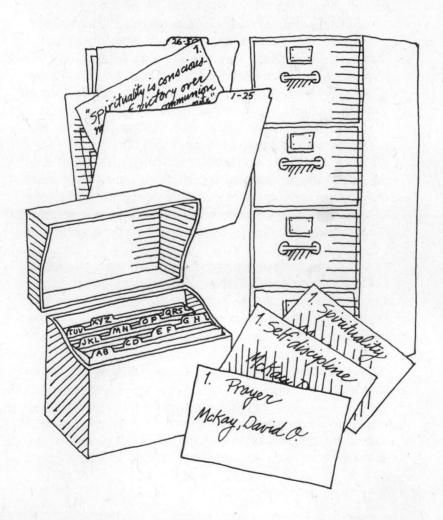

under Priesthood Order, Marriage, Obedience, as well as Stewardship. If it were listed under stewardship only, I might forget its significant application to marriage.

b. The system doesn't require much time to set it up and keep it current. All you need to do is pick up one item to be filed, place a number on it in the upper right-hand corner, make out the index cards, and place it in the file folder. By doing this each time you find something you wish to keep, think of the wealth of material you can file in five or ten years.

c. The system allows for materials of all shapes and sizes. Not only can the master file direct you to items in your filing cabinet, but it can also remind you of special passages in books on your bookshelves (listed by chapter and page on the index cards), games in a cabinet, posters, maps, or any other over-sized items that don't fit into the filing cabinet. It is also a handy place to note where you keep a list of storage items, such as clothing for children to grow into, holiday decorations, carpet and wallpaper remnants, and other miscellaneous things that are located in your attic, basement, garage, or elsewhere. In other words, a master file can serve as a reference source for anything in your home.

I have a schoolteacher friend who was frustrated because she had many teaching supplies at school as well as in her home. Her problem was solved when she listed all of her supplies in a master file. The next time Halloween came around, for example, she just pulled out the Halloween card and was instantly reminded of all her decorations and materials and where they were located.

d. This system allows for some items to be grouped together. If you have certain things that are always used together, they could be placed in one envelope and given one number. Decorating ideas for your home, roadmaps, warranties, and instructions for operating appliances are types of "like" items that can easily be grouped together. I have a folder for Old Testament pictures, one for New Testament, one for principles of the gospel, one for nature, one for family and holiday pictures, etc.

In one drawer of my filing cabinet I also have a box with ideas for children's rainy day fun. There is a small box for birthday party ideas, another for bridal and baby shower favors, games and invitations. Whenever I get a clever invitation, favor, placecard, or such from a party, I bring it home—gumdrops and all—secure it in a plastic bag, and drop it in the labeled container in my file for future inspiration.

e. Indexes to Church magazines fit into the same system; that is, all references are classified according to title, author, and subjects. These indexes are available at nominal cost from the Church Magazine Office, 50 East North Temple, Salt Lake City, Utah 84150. I store the magazines in cardboard containers (you may use cereal or soap boxes, or special boxes for this purpose are also available inexpensively from the Church Magazine Office) and keep the indexes in a looseleaf binder near my master file. Of course, an article that particularly impresses you can also be listed in your master file according to magazine, year, month, page.

f. This master file system provides a great idea source. Frequently one of our children will report he's been asked to give a talk. The most difficult part of a talk is finding a subject to talk about, so we just thumb through the master file and within a few minutes he's selected a subject and is enthusiastically developing it. I usually flip through my master file for each lesson or talk I must give, and usually find just the right stories, poems, scriptural references, and thoughts.

g. Anyone in the family can make use of the file.

I keep a small card in front of the file upon which family members jot down what they have taken from the file to make certain that it's returned. It's easy to borrow something from the file, use it, and then tuck it into a book and forget to return it to the file; the "check-out" card helps avoid this.

The master file system as explained here can be developed and refined for any home. One word of caution, however: be highly selective in what you file. Don't file something just because it's in print. Make certain that it's worth keeping and using again. The wastebasket should play an important role in your project.

Here are some questions I've been asked about this system, with my answers:

*Question:* Do you place more than one entry on each index card?

*Answer:* I do, while some people do not. Obviously, some cards are fuller than others. Also, by listing more than one entry on a card, I find it is much faster to see what is available and how much material is on file on a particular subject. This also greatly reduces the number of cards needed in the master file.

*Question:* How do you handle bulky items for filing?

*Answer:* Usually bulky items, such as books, are left on a shelf with a reference to them in the master file. Some small booklets are placed directly in my filing cabinet, however.

*Question:* What about very small items?

*Answer:* If something is so small it might become lost in the manila folder, I either recopy it on a large piece of paper or card or paste it on a larger sheet of paper or card.

*Question:* Do you number over again with each drawer in your filing cabinet?

*Answer:* Yes, I do. Otherwise the digits get too high. I handle this by numbering each drawer with a roman numeral—I, II, III, IV. Then the file items go from 1 to 750 in each drawer.

*Question:* Are you ever unable to locate something because you can't remember the author or title and are vague about the specific subjects?

*Answer:* Rarely. When this happens, I quickly flip through the master file until I find it.

*Question:* Do you file only gospel-oriented items?

*Answer:* Yes, but to me the gospel is all-inclusive. Remember, we seek after anything that is "virtuous, lovely, or of good report or praiseworthy." I do have a separate file for my recipes, however, and my husband keeps a separate financial file.

*Question:* Should children be encouraged to start files?

*Answer:* Yes, definitely! I started my file as a teenager, and a young girl in our neighborhood was excited last Christmas to receive filing supplies from her parents as a gift.

# 4

## *Be More Than Efficient:*
## *Be Effective!*

*"Our success depends not only
upon the use of our time,
but also on the use of its
by-product, the odd moment."*
—Arthur Brisbane

**E**fficiency, according to the *World Book Dictionary*, means to be able to produce the effect wanted without waste of time or energy. The same dictionary describes effectiveness as the power to produce results.

It's well understood that efficiency for efficiency's sake is a thoughtless, empty, machine-like approach to a task. There is much more to life than seeing if the bed can be made in one minute rather than two—unless the minute saved (plus others similarly gained) can be used to improve the quality of your life and that of those around you.

To me, the purpose of efficiency is to do what you have to do quickly and well so there is time to do what you *want* to do. We all want to be more than the family janitor who merely cleans up around the house. We want to have time and strength to add the meaningful touches to our families and homes and to be *effective* in all facets of our lives. Here are some specific suggestions for efficiency that can lead to effectiveness.

1. *Don't make two jobs out of one.*

Too often people carelessly or thoughtlessly make work for themselves. This can be avoided if a few simple precautions are taken, such as the following:

a. Don't make a mess if you can avoid it.

b. Guard against unnecessary spills.

c. Why toss candy wrappers or the like in a drawer and then have to pick them up later and dispose of them? Throw them away in the first place!

d. Avoid misplacing something only to have to look for it later. Have a place for everything and keep everything in its place.

  e. After removing ice cubes from the tray, immediately refill the tray with water and return it to the freezer. Setting it down on the kitchen counter makes it a likely target for crumbs and sticky spots, resulting in a cleaning job.

  f. Be sure the area has been wiped clean when you put down water pitchers, jam bottles, butter plates, and lids in the working area of the kitchen.

  g. When you're making sandwiches, putting up lunches, baking, preparing dinner, or other such tasks, confine the mess to one area as far as possible to reduce the cleaning-up problem.

2. *Use things and save yourself.*

There are many material things in the world, but there's only one you! Allow these things to serve and save you. You deserve the tools of your trade just as much as does any professional person. Many kitchen gadgets can save you time and energy. Some of my favorite ones are:

- wire whisk
- rubber scraper
- kitchen shears
- tomato slicer
- egg slicer
- basting syringe
- melon baller
- tongs (regular, barbecue, spaghetti, and fruit bottling types)
- vegetable scrapers, cutters, graters, dicers, etc.
- "Punch 'n Cover" for canned milk
- apple corer-slicer
- "Wonder Cup" for measuring shortening peanut butter (an ice cream scoop may also be used)

Good utility items, such as brooms, dustpans, mops, dust cloths, pail, sponges, and clothes, are indispensable to housekeeping. New and improved cleaning agents can also save you much time and effort. And small and large appliances can save hundreds of hours a year and do the work better than human hands.

3. *Work smarter, not harder.*

Many homemakers work hard enough, but they could be much more effective if they would learn to work smarter. For example:

a. Clean hairbrush and combs (after removing excess hair) by tossing them into the washer along with the regular wash.

b. Cook in double batches and freeze pastries, casseroles, pizzas, sauces, and other dishes for quick future meals.

c. Consider the fabric content label as well as the price when you select clothing and fabrics. Don't waste your time by ironing more than is absolutely necessary.

d. Have telephone extensions with long cords located in working areas so kitchens can be cleared, clothing can be folded or mended, or other quiet projects can be carried on while you talk on the phone.

e. Never make two trips to the store when one will do. (Use your head and save your heels is still great advice!)

f. Have a broom and dustpan upstairs as well as downstairs, if you live on two levels; and don't forget an extra set for the garage or carport. Having extra sets of utility items can save time and steps.

g. Keep paper and a pencil in your food storage area for jotting down items that need to be replaced.

h. Place spice containers alphabetically on shelves. It's also smart to alphabetize soup cans.

i. Wipe off salt and pepper shakers, spice cans, flavoring extract bottles, and other such items before returning them to shelves.

j. Have linen colors (sheets, pillow cases, and towels) that are specifically used for each room.

k. Work out some kind of family incentive plan for avoiding spills at the table.

l. If space is available, have some sort of locker

constructed in an entryway for children's coats, caps, gloves, boots, lunch pails, and school supplies. If there is space, have a separate locker for each child.

m. A padded board placed over part of the bath-tub (we used one-third of an old door) makes an ideal changing table for the baby, with water, diaper pail, and supplies handy. The board can easily be lifted off and set aside when someone wants to bathe.

n. Use drawstring bags made from nylon net to keep children's socks and other small items together in the laundry. Clothing may be washed and dried in the bags, as long as they are not filled too full. Assign a different color bag to each child (I find the colors easy to remember if they match the children's bed-rooms). Make four or five bags for each child: one for white clothes, another for colored, and others for spares while some are being washed and dried. (Stu-dents living in dormitories find this is a helpful idea for keeping their socks and lingerie from becoming mixed up with those of their roommates.) Make a rule that dirty clothes are to be placed in the proper bags; then if a child fails to place his soiled socks in his bag and to put the bag in the clothes hamper or chute, his socks won't get washed—and he'll quickly learn to cooperate. Note: Commercial nylon net bags with zipper openings are available at notions counters in department stores, if you don't want to make your own.

Laundry efficiency can also be achieved if the utility area is arranged for the greatest and most efficient use. Containers that we call clothes baskets can be placed on shelves above the washer, dryer, and folding counter, for example, for freshly laundered clothing. (We use plastic dishpans purchased at a discount store.) When the baskets are full, the children themselves take their baskets to their rooms, place the contents in their drawers, and return the baskets to the utility room. This keeps the utility room free from stacks of clothing and saves the homemaker many steps in running from room to room with clothing.

4. *Don't let things stack up.*

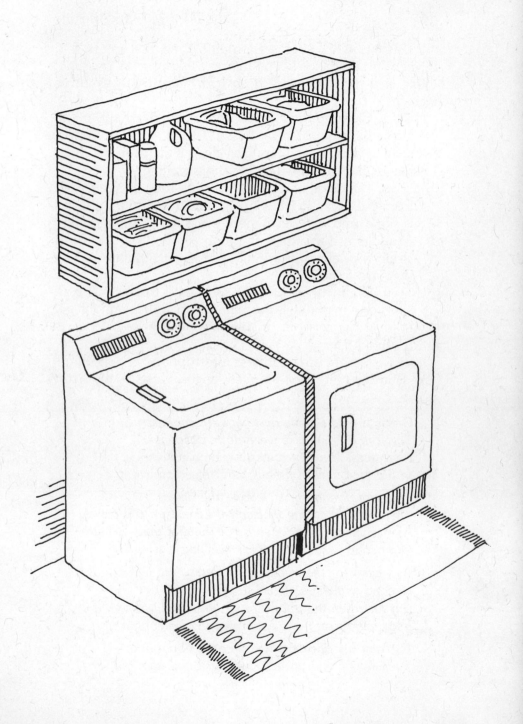

Leftover work seems to multiply, so the smart and efficient homemaker keeps things as current as possible. (This is a psychological help too.) Some suggestions include:

a. Clear up the kitchen after every meal and cooking or baking project; a messy kitchen is almost impossible to work in, and trying to clean it up when the mess has accumulated is terribly discouraging.

b. Fold clothes just as soon as they are removed from the dryer. It takes only a few minutes' time if this is done, and with permanent press items, unnecessary wrinkles are avoided. It's also a much bigger job if batches of clothing are allowed to accumulate before they are folded.

c. Clean up promptly after any project. If not, someone might spill the paint, or a toddler might get hold of the scissors or marking pen.

5. *Avoid flitting.*

At best, there are countless interruptions in a mother's day. But don't interrupt yourself, as this verse by my sister points out:

*One morning I woke and began resolutely*
*To work till my tasks were done absolutely.*
*I decided I would not waste even a minute—*
*In the race against time, I determined to win it.*

*I started all right, first clearing the dishes,*
*Then noticed it time to clean the bowl for the fishes.*
*As I reached for the cleanser I thought that I'd better*
*Grab soap flakes as well for washing a sweater.*

*As I went for the sweater, I saw that the bed*
*Needed straightening, so stopped to do that instead.*
*But just then the phone rang, and while answering it,*
*I saw plants on the sill that needed watering a bit.*

*So went my day, and I worked till bone tired;*
*Then happy and proud, I sat back and admired.*

*But taking stock of my home, my joy soon diminished;*
*Everything was started, but nothing was finished.*

    —Donette V. Ockey

In addition to following through on household tasks, make certain also that you stick to projects until they're completed. No matter how clever or creative you might be, it's to no avail until you actually produce something. As someone has said, "Reaching home plate with one idea is better than letting three ideas die on base!"

    6.*Think in dimes.*

Several years ago I took two of our little girls, ages six and four, to the store, gave them a dollar bill, and then, at their request, left them alone in the toy department to pick out a birthday gift for another little sister. A few minutes later I returned, eager to see their selection. But they hand't yet looked for a gift; instead of the dollar bill, the six-year-old had ten dimes clutched in her little hand. I asked her why. She replied, "We went to the cashier and changed the dollar because we could think better in dimes. Now we're ready to look for the gift."

How often in my own life have I had three or four lessons to prepare and several speaking assignments to give and found I couldn't think about one because of the other! I felt so frustrated by all of them that I found it difficult to focus on one until I broke down the assignments in my mind and had dimes to work with rather than the dollar. I've found also that listing things to do in an agenda book, as described in the chapter "On Getting Things Done," helps me greatly.

Too much to do—too many things in your life or on your mind at one time—can result in a major letdown in efficiency and effectiveness. Don't let your life become too involved. It *is* a lot easier to think (and work) in dimes!

    7. *Be mindful of the minute.*

Suggestions for improving efficiency could go on and

on. In fact, entire books have been written on the subject. Let me recommend just one more, which people of accomplishment practice: Use your time well!

I'll always remember an incident in our mission home office in Holland when a missionary was bemoaning the fact that his weekly letter home was greatly overdue, and he just didn't know when he would be able to find the time to write. During the time in which he was pacing the floor and complaining, another missionary quietly sat down and had his letter home well underway!

Many of us who think our days and our lives are full would find there is additional time if we were more mindful of the minutes and learned the value of the word *while:* set the table while the water is coming to a boil; toss the salad while the meat is roasting; wipe off the refrigerator while chatting on the phone; read the front page of the newspaper while the family is gathering for an outing; sew on a button while waiting for the dryer to stop tumbling the clothes; file an item while waiting for that ride to come along; start loading the dishwasher while the family is coming to the table; read an article while waiting in the car for a child to run an errand; study a lesson while under the hair dryer. As Henry Haddow said, "The real secret of how to use time is to pack it as you would your luggage: filling the small spaces with small things."

# 5
## *On Getting Things Done*

*Being organized
is not a matter of following
a schedule through the day,
but rather one of fitting a schedule
to the day.*

A faithful Latter-day Saint woman is just about as busy as a person can be. Her life is filled to overflowing with being a devoted wife, a loving mother, and a good homemaker. She is also a dedicated church worker, a thoughtful neighbor, a gracious hostess, a supporter of school and community affairs, and carries on a continuing program of self-development. This would be impossible were it not for some special attitudes and abilities. Let's consider some of these helps.

First, ours is an eternal perspective; we are building homes to last forever.

We are a service-oriented rather than a pleasure-seeking people. We thrive on being constructively engaged in helping our families and others.

We feel, as Alfred Lord Tennyson expressed in his poem "Sir Galahad": "My strength is as the strength of ten, because my heart is pure." Through living as the gospel teaches us and remaining close to our Father in heaven, we do find purity of heart and a peace of mind that brings strength and energy to match our responsibilities.

We are an idea-sharing people, and it's ideas that give us fuel for our self-starters.

In the next few pages we'll look at some ideas about getting things done. More specifically, we'll talk about getting organized, working to a system, and planning ahead. When we do, we are the master, rather than the victim, of our work, our day, and ultimately our life.

Sometimes people are confused about what organization really is and get its meaning mixed up with the clock or calendar. Actually, organization doesn't necessarily have anything to do with either. One dictionary says that organization is "to put into working order; get together and arrange." Related to homemaking, this means we take the duties of our day, as many and varied as they may be, and arrange them in a working order. (The following chapter, "Walking Through a Week," will have a more detailed plan for this.)

In attempting this, we shouldn't be overly concerned if we find ourselves a little behind. Actually, we can be two hours behind with our work or even two weeks behind and still be organized. Contrary to what many people think, keeping up with the clock doesn't have to be the measuring stick for being organized. Rather, this is the test: *If you are in control of the situation, you are organized. If the situation is in control of you, you are not organized.*

Being organized is really the easy way to live. It frees one from frustration and frenzy, confusion and conflicts, tension and turmoil, pressures and problems.

Nevertheless, some people still work against the laws of organization. This reminds me of a woman who managed her home quite poorly. She was always behind with her work, and everything she did was at the expense of something else. For instance, during the breakfast hour, when she should have been preparing and serving food and helping every family member off to a good start, she would be frantically pressing a blouse for her daughter or ironing a shirt for her husband to wear that day. In fact, her husband once commented that he had never known what it was like to wear a cool shirt! This is living from "board to back" and certainly is an awkward, inefficient way to do things.

The first step in getting organized is:

PLAN AHEAD

Advance planning can double or even triple your accomplishments. The old cliché holds true: use your head and save your heels.

One woman confessed that she was ready to fold the diapers one morning when she suddenly realized that she hadn't even washed and dried them yet. Perhaps this is a little far-fetched, but there really are women who find it difficult to plan their day so that it comes out even. Fortunately, most women sort of innately know how to plan, just as they know how much salt to put on the potatoes or when to check the baby, but once in awhile there is a woman who has to consciously cultivate this extra sense.

I've had a very special friend ever since grade school. We were married about the same time, and shortly afterwards she and her husband invited Hank and me to dinner. I was eager to go—and also interested in how she, a new bride, would manage a formal dinner. (Some brides do have problems, you know. I heard of one who made a tuna fish casserole but forgot to put in the tuna fish!) I needn't have worried. The table was beautifully set with her wedding crystal and china, and dinner was served on time. All of the foods that should have been hot were hot and those that should have been cold were cold, and everything was absolutely delicious.

After the meal I helped carry some of the food back into the kitchen. Again I was impressed. Her kitchen was in complete order. Preparatory dishes and utensils had been washed and put away. Her countertop was wiped off. Even the sink was clean. I could tell she had managed well throughout the entire project. Then I noticed a little list taped to the cabinet door that read something like this:

3:30　Roll out rolls
4:00　Put roast in oven
5:15　Put potatoes on to cook
5:30　Slice tomatoes for salad
5:45　Put rolls in oven
6:00　Dinner

That was the answer to her very successful dinner party.

She had literally planned everything in advance.

We've been in their home a number of times since for other dinners, and each one has been just as beautifully prepared and served as that first one. But I've never seen a list since. A few years ago I asked her about it. She laughed; she had forgotten all about the list and had never realized that I had even noticed it. She replied, "I don't keep a list like that any more. I now know how to give dinner parties." Then, after a moment's hesitation, she continued, "Actually, I still keep sketchy lists along with my recipes of the menu, and when to let things thaw, rise, or cook, because with all the distractions of the children and the telephone, it's easy to forget. I don't want the guests arriving at the door just as I remember that the rolls are still in the refrigerator and require three hours to raise. It would also be embarrassing to bid the guests good-night and suddenly remember that I'd forgotten to serve the salad."

That's planning in advance. Perhaps a detailed list is needed in some cases, and brief notes are sufficient in others. Maybe the plan is only in your head. Whatever the case, it's planning in advance that makes for success for everything from sightseeing in a strange city to running errands about town.

Step number two is:

HAVE A FLEXIBLE SCHEDULE

A schedule, like a road map, tells you where you are going. It's a road for your work to run on. There may be some detours, bumps, or stopovers along the way (some of these can be more interesting than the road and very worthwhile), but to eventually reach your destination, you've got to get back on the road.

Technically speaking, a mother's schedule isn't much of a schedule at all, with little people around causing her to constantly adjust and rearrange it. It's more like a series of plans or goals toward which she keeps working. A schedule is much like a basic dress pattern. It may need lengthening or shortening, to be taken in or let out, depending on the needs of the day. One way or another, it must be altered and accessorized to fit the situation.

In carrying out my plans I find it disastrous, with eight active children and a constantly ringing telephone, to try to chart my course by determining that I'll start this task at 8:00, then be ready for this other one at 8:10, and for another one at 8:30, and so on. That's an open invitation to frustration and failure. Instead, I find it much more realistic to plan in this manner: By noon I hope to have certain things accomplished, and by the end of the day, certain other duties will be done. Before the week is out, I intend to have such and such finished, and by the end of the month, one or more special projects should be completed.

The purpose of organization is not so a woman is able to follow a schedule right down the line; anyone can disregard the world around her and do that. The real test of an effective home manager is to be able to work in, rearrange, tuck in here, eliminate there, add here, make a split-second adjustment at some other point, until all the goals have been reached.

As you make your plans, may I suggest a half dozen or so things that would be good to keep in mind as you determine your daily, weekly, monthly, and longer-range goals.

A mother of eleven was once asked how she managed her home. She answered, "I operate on a system of selected neglect." She has a point. There are times in many households when everything can't be done all the time. Morning sickness, a new baby, house guests, three children down with the chicken pox, holidays—such situations demand changes in the daily routine.

When major disruptions come along, I find that if I just lay the foundation and do only the essentials, the house looks all right on the surface, it still runs fairly smoothly, and there is time to cope with the unusual. It's more important to have clean baby bottles than it is to have clean windows!

In other words, at such times you need to shift into a lower gear—to take things at a slower pace. Instead of bemoaning the fact that you're off schedule, merely change your schedule to fit the situation. Plan only what you can realistically do. Referring to the mother of eleven, if you select carefully enough, then what you're neglecting won't matter for awhile.

It's vital to take out some "wife insurance" along the way. By this I mean you should have some time for yourself and your own personal refreshment and relaxation. That's the purpose behind schedules and plans. You make things happen; you don't let life run you—you run your life.

To me this special time is a few minutes at the typewriter, putting on paper the thoughts running through my mind, or working my way through the correspondence and papers that constantly accumulate at my desk, or reading or studying, or visiting with a good friend.

Other women unwind at the piano or in the flower garden, with a nap or playing tennis. Whatever you choose, a few uninterrupted minutes each day puts your perspective in better order and steels you for the stress and strain of the rest of the day. With this private time closely guarded, your public time can be much more effective. In my case, if I miss it for several days in a row, I feel myself gradually coming "unglued." With it, I can be bigger than any problem.

It's also important to plan time for your husband. Talking things over, exchanging experiences of the day, going for a walk, having a date—this is a must for both of you.

Children require a great deal of special time from you. If you don't plan and take the time to read to them, they'll soon be off to college and you still won't have gotten around to it. Unless you plan a specific time to visit a new neighbor with a loaf of freshly baked bread or a plate of cookies, it's likely she'll soon be an old neighbor and you'll feel it's too late.

Another thought to keep in mind as you plan your day is to go the second mile. This familiar advice stems from biblical days when a Roman soldier could require a Jew to carry his belongings for one mile; this was the law, and the Jew went as a slave. Of course, that mile was a long, hot, dusty, and thirst-provoking one.

Even though the second-mile custom is well known, many of us still limit ourselves to the bleakness and misery of the first mile. Housewives, for instance, sometimes do just what they absolutely have to do around the home, and no more. No wonder they feel enslaved and resent their long, dull days.

But such doesn't have to be the case. Fortunately, many homemakers have discovered the second mile. Not only do they dust off the tabletop, but they choose to make it a second-mile experience by also gracing it with a vase of flowers. They don't just feed their families—they serve them appetizing, nutritious meals. They have learned that it is much more exciting and rewarding to teach children than to just tend them. They don't just keep house; they make a home.

Now, don't get the impression that the first mile can be eliminated. Regardless of one's work, whether it's home-making, teaching school, dentistry, painting houses, or selling, there is some routine drudgery that has to be handled each day. But the way to conquer it is to get through it as efficiently and effectively as possible. A dull job slackly done becomes twice as dull, whereas a dull job that you try to do just as well as you possibly can becomes half as dull. It's the little bit extra, the special effort, the second mile that transforms a tedious duty into a satisfying experience.

Happy, rewarding homemaking results from doing well

what you have to do and being able to manage successfully enough also to do what you choose to do—to add the special touches that make a house a home, a job a joy, a group of people living together an eternal family unit. One of the greatest blessings a woman can have is to find fulfillment in her home, and this fulfillment lies in direct proportion to the number of second miles she is able to travel in her day.

While participating in an Education Week program sponsored by the Church Education System, I was approached by a bishop and asked if I planned to talk to the women about getting up on time. I responded that I would mention it, if he wished. He said, "Hit it hard, sister, hit it hard! Some very serious problems in our ward stem from mothers who just don't get going in the mornings." Make certain you've got mind over mattress, so to speak, and get an early start each day. If arising early makes the day seem too long, take a short nap after lunch. That hour isn't nearly as vital as the one before breakfast. Never forget how exhausting that extra hour's sleep can ultimately be. An ounce of morning is worth a pound of afternoon.

A newspaper columnist who features advice on family living received a letter from a woman who was despairing the fact that a man works from sun to sun, but a woman's work is never done. He responded, "Dear Madam: Your problem is poor management." I'll bet she was infuriated! He didn't understand a woman's world at all, she felt. Why, there is always more work to be done. She knew that. I believe, however, that the writer meant it this way: If you plan your work and then work your plan, by nighttime you should *feel* through. There may be mending that needs doing, but that wasn't on the agendum for today—that is scheduled for next Tuesday. Therefore, don't concern yourself about the mending now. Remember, being organized is partly a mental attitude.

Technically speaking, you can never have everything

completely caught up at one moment. There's always a glass that someone just used and put in the sink, or a wet diaper on the baby that just had to be changed. But you don't run to the kitchen to wash every glass as it's used or to the washer with every used diaper. After you've done today's batch of diapers, others are placed in the diaper pail until tomorrow. That's what diaper pails are for.

Every weekday at our house I completely empty the clothes chute and wash one or more batches of white whites, one of semi-whites, and one of colored clothes. Then I am through washing for the day. I don't go back later to the clothes chute, look at the pile of soiled clothing building up again, and moan, "Oh, I'm never caught up. There it is again." I know that what is there is tomorrow's wash; I've already done today's. If you follow this philosophy, you'll like yourself (and your housework) much better and you'll be a lot pleasanter to live with.

Here's another thought to keep in mind as you plan: "It takes two days to keep the Sabbath day holy," a wise homemaker stated. And it does!

You've probably sung with young children in Junior Sunday School the little hymn "Saturday Is a Special Day." If it can't be Saturday, then it has to be Friday for making Sunday preparations: doing the marketing, washing and pressing clothes, cleaning the house, polishing shoes, shampooing hair, and preparing food so only minimum effort is required on Sunday.

The Lord said it this way: "Six days shalt thou labour and do all thy work." Many women who have the best-cared-for homes and the happiest families and who are ahead rather than behind in their work honor Sunday as the Lord's day and do their work the other six days. On the other hand, those who cook, clean, wash, shop, iron, and mend seven days a week may find life a miserable grind and feel themselves completely wearing down. They can hardly face Monday morning and "the same old thing all over again." They miss the refreshing and needed break Sunday should offer in the routine of their lives.

Now, no typical Latter-day Saint Sunday is a day of rest, what with meetings to attend, Church assignments to fulfill, toddlers to keep quiet during meetings, and guidance to give growing children in aligning their activities with the spirit of the day. But it's the Lord's work we're attending to, not our own. That makes all the difference!

Just as one of the fringe benefits to tithing is to help us budget our money and have it go farther as a result, so honoring the Sabbath can aid us in working out a more effective schedule and managing our time more satisfactorily.

If you are already committed to this way of life, then you are reaping the benefits. If not, resolve now to honor the Sabbath day by thoroughly planning and preparing for it in advance. You'll be impressed with all you can accomplish and the good, up-to-date feeling that can be yours. Above all, you and your family will receive spiritual strength in the process.

Always remember, in carrying out your plans, what is a *minute,* more or less. For example, don't fuss at children to hurry as they get in and out of cars, up and down from the table, and so forth. The fifteen seconds saved are hardly worth the tension and pressure that is built up. To be effectively lived, life is a continuing process of weighing values. A meaningful visit with Daddy may be of much greater value to a child than getting to bed right on time. Sometimes it's better to do the important rather than the urgent task. Make certain that you're in control of the schedule, not that the schedule is controlling you!

Thus far we have discussed the first two steps toward organization: (1) plan ahead, and (2) have a flexible schedule. Let's look now at the third one:

BE A LIST MAKER: GET THE NOTEBOOK HABIT

I can vividly recall a canyon party I attended as a little girl where no one had a very necessary can opener except my mother. And she was prepared with it (and everything else) because she had made up a list and then packed accordingly. Others in the party kidded her about her lists, but even though I was a young girl, I quickly saw the value of them.

Since then, as I've observed people, and particularly during the years when I've been closely involved in helping them in their home management, I've realized that making lists is one of the smartest things a person can do.

To me, a list of things to do is the only type of "pep pill" I could ever take, and seeing items on that list crossed off is the perfect kind of "tranquilizer" to me. To me, lists are highly therapeutic. I firmly believe that the Lord wants us to learn to motivate ourselves naturally and then be able to calm ourselves from within. We should use will power, not pill power.

It can be highly satisfying to cross off completed items at the end of the day. This reminds me of a neighbor who related that she was crossing off items on her list one evening when she realized she had accomplished several other things that weren't on the list—so she wrote them down just to be able to cross them off!

It's human nature, however, to make the mistake of evaluating a list unfairly. We tend to dwell on what has *not* been completed rather than on what *has* been accomplished. Don't let two or three unfinished tasks detract from the satisfaction of the ten things that were completed.

Many husbands appreciate their wives' keeping a list on the family bulletin board for them—a list of minor repair jobs, man-size chores, and outside activities that need a husband's attention. Then when he has a few minutes' time he can tackle a project. This prevents a wife's nagging, and as one man put it, "It's terrible to go through life 'listless.'"

But in most cases, lists in and of themselves are not sufficient, as this verse explains:

*My husband, with his day's work done,*
*Says, "You should organize!*
*Be more efficient in your work!*
*Make plans, dear; visualize!"*

*I try to follow his advice.*
*I schedule—he insists.*
*And I could be efficient, too,*
*If I could just find my lists!*

Ever since I was a missionary in the Netherlands, I've carried a small 4″ x 5″ agenda book that contains my lists—not routine things to do, but the extras. In other words, I don't list first-mile duties, just second-mile projects.

# 6
# *Walking Through A Week*

*A look at one
homemaker's schedule
for a week*

I like to think that the Lord made a special point of creating everyone different, and that no teacher or parent should try to remake everyone alike. Certainly it's not the purpose of this book to produce carbon-copy homemakers. Our life-styles are delightfully different, and the best way may well be your way.

But if you are looking for solutions and ideas, let's walk through a week together. At least the principles may apply.

Most important, I feel, is to begin and end my day with prayer. An old English proverb reminds us, "Prayer should be the key to the day and the lock to the night."

First, I like to wake up to an orderly house. I don't want to do yesterday's work today! Toys, clothing, and items for snacks and projects from the night before should have been put away before bedtime. In this way, I'm ahead before I've even put one foot on the floor.

Next, I get up at about 6:30. (If you lose an hour in the morning, you'll spend the rest of the day looking for it.) If I'm behind in my work or want to complete a project, I may arise an hour or so earlier than usual. For me, this prime time between five and six o'clock is worth many hours any other hour of the day. We all joke about needing an eight-day week. This is the way to make it happen!

For many years the first activity of my day was to feed the baby, but now I start by making the bed and dressing partially while my husband washes and shaves. Then I wash and complete my dressing, comb my hair, and apply make-up. Often there is time to tidy up the master bedroom and thus as I leave the room, our area of home is in order for the day. Otherwise I have to go back and do that later. Then I assist the four-year-old with his dressing (he can do everything but tie his shoes now) and bedmaking (he can't do that alone as yet).

Perhaps prior to helping him I've started some cereal steaming or at this point I'll make other preparations for breakfast. (During the years of feeding and changing babies and helping several little ones start their day, I was fortunate to have a husband who enjoyed cooking breakfast. At least he knew I needed some help, and he preferred cooking over changing diapers.) Things are a lot easier now that my children are able to do more for themselves, and I can handle preparing breakfast alone, though I love it when on a Saturday or holiday Hank voluntarily stirs up some french toast batter and starts cooking.

We've discovered that it takes a child about two minutes to dress before breakfast and about two hours to dress afterwards, so we gain on the day by requiring that they all wash and dress before coming for family prayer and breakfast. Then we go about our individual duties. My husband leaves for work, and I start to sort clothes and run them through the washer.

The children proceed with their chores after putting their bedrooms in order. Divided eight ways, there isn't more than five minutes' work for anyone. These duties include feeding the cat and the dog, cleaning up the breakfast table and dishes, polishing bathrooms, vacuuming traffic areas, dusting furniture (done every other day at our house), emptying wastebaskets as needed, putting up lunches, and so forth.

This is also an excellent hour for the children to practice their music. (Before breakfast is even better!) Many music teachers claim that for many children, half an hour of practice before school is worth more than an hour after school.

I take my turns driving our children and others in the neighborhood to high school. Fortunately, we're within walking distance of the elementary and junior high schools. As the children leave for school or begin to play, I spend about another hour puttering around, completing the washing, folding clothes, and doing other small chores. Thus, by 10:00 (give or take half an hour) I have the foundation laid and am ready to start building.

To be honest, however, this is an oversimplification of things. There is almost always a crisis with which we have to cope: we wake to find a child has had a nosebleed during the night; a last-minute phone call informs us that the car pool isn't coming by and I have to make an emergency trip to school; or a heavy snowstorm sends the children outside with shovels and all the inside duties are left to me. But if you're organized and have things under control, an emergency doesn't usually throw you too far off course.

Often, advance dinner preparations take some time in the morning. There are lots of telephone calls to be made, but with a long cord, I always include a nearby project, such as folding clothes, sewing on a button, or wiping woodwork, while I talk. We have many visitors too, and they are always welcome. There is usually an hour or so for some other duties; then I serve lunch to whoever is home and clear up the kitchen again.

Whatever my activities and errands have been during the day, I make a special effort to be home when the children return from school. I visit with them, go over their papers, and run them on errands. Chauffering is a big thing in a mother's life, I've found. Next to toilet-training a child, I believe launching one of them with a driver's license with limited use of the family car is the greatest step in relieving a mother! On the other hand, driving with children presents an ideal opportunity to talk with them.

This time spent with children after school is extremely precious and important, as the following poem indicates:

*It may be French provincial,*
*Or perhaps of Colonial style,*
*Spanish, or Early American,*
*With carpeting by the mile.*

*It may have elegant draperies*
*And gadgets everywhere.*
*But if mother's not home*
*When the children come in,*
*That house will feel empty and bare.*

*Perhaps you use second-hand dressers,*
*And some walls are a little bit bare;*
*No one will notice any of this*
*If good cooking smells fill the air.*

*So even though the carpet is worn*
*And your plans are just finished in part,*
*If mother is home when the children come in,*
*That home will have beauty and heart.*

*—Donette V. Ockey*

After I have greeted the children and they are busy with homework or other after-school activities, I complete the dinner preparations from a menu made out on a weekly basis. This way, I'm never distressed over what to eat tonight, and we have a much better meal when things are planned rather than thrown together. I can coordinate menus with busy days and out-of-the house days so there is always a nourishing meal ready at dinnertime.

A woman at the supermarket was heard to say, "I'm sick and tired of planning meals. I'm just going to kick the shelf and cook whatever falls down." Almost every homemaker feels this way occasionally. What she needs is some new ideas—a recipe exchange with a neighbor or a few minutes browsing through the pages of a tantalizing cookbook.

What about your cooking? Are you only a first-miler

here—just barely getting a meal together—or do you go the second mile and let dinners at your house reflect real interest?

This reminds me of the man whose family had suddenly shrunk in size due to marriage and missions. A young friend of his who had recently married asked him how it seemed to have the household diminish so quickly. "The worst problem is the meals," he replied. "My wife forgets that the boys are gone, and she cooks enough to feed the army." "Don't feel too bad," the young man consoled him. "My wife cooks as if she's feeding the enemy."

Seriously, it really isn't too difficult to be a good cook. I'll always remember the advice from a friend who said that if you can read, you can cook—provided you read the right recipes. It's smart to constantly upgrade your recipes, have a good cookbook collection, and be alert to new ideas in magazines and newspapers. Remember, the eye is the first to feast, so serve food attractively. Make certain your meals are well balanced. Nature is an artist. I've found that a dinner that follows pleasing texture and color combinations almost automatically includes nutrients from the basic four food group. Keep in mind that the delicious dinners can be more a matter of know-how than of time and money.

Now, on to the after-dinner activities. A neighbor once told me that it was her policy never to do any work after the sun went down. (Her family and home showed it, too!) What is work, anyway? Mark Twain defined it this way: "Work is something a body is obliged to do. Play consists of something a body is not obliged to do."

Luckily for most of us, there are many things—even though they are productive and resemble work—that we enjoy doing. Most of my evenings are filled with these types of activities: bedtime routines with younger children, visits with older children and my husband, reading, studying, special projects, watching television on a highly selective basis (which means almost never in my case—I'd rather write a book), and leaving the house in order for the night. Of course, we do enjoy going out occasionally for social activities.

This in no way includes all of the duties in a homemaker's day. Compiling a complete list would be quite impossible. I do appreciate one company's attempt to calculate a wife's worth, however, and feel complimented by the monetary value they have attached to each of our responsibilities.

*WHAT'S A WIFE WORTH? IT CAN BE CALCULATED!*

| Jobs Performed | Hours Per Week | Rate Per Hour | Value Per Week |
|---|---|---|---|
| Nursemaid | 44.5 | $2.00 | $ 89.00 |
| Housekeeper | 17.5 | 3.25 | 56.88 |
| Cook | 13.1 | 3.25 | 42.58 |
| Dishwasher | 6.2 | 2.00 | 12.40 |
| Laundress | 5.9 | 2.50 | 14.75 |
| Food Buyer | 3.3 | 3.50 | 11.55 |
| Gardener | 2.3 | 3.00 | 6.90 |
| Chauffeur | 2.0 | 3.25 | 6.50 |
| Maintenance Man | 1.7 | 3.00 | 5.10 |
| Seamstress | 1.3 | 3.25 | 4.22 |
| Dietician | 1.2 | 4.50 | 5.40 |
| Practical Nurse | 0.6 | 3.75 | 2.25 |
| TOTAL | 99.6 | -- | $257.53 |
| *ANNUAL SERVICE VALUE* | | | $13,391.56 |

Source: Chase Manhattan Bank, New York, N.Y.

So much for the daily doings. Now let's move on to weekly appointments and meetings, such as Relief Society.

Ironing is a once-a-week job at our house, though it is constantly on the decrease. I'm grateful I was sent to earth during the permanent-press era! I'm happy to be relieved of most of this tedious chore and to be able to move on to things of much greater importance.

Mending too is a weekly task, unless I've gotten it all done except the sewing machine work while talking on the telephone.

I go to the market once a week, and once every four

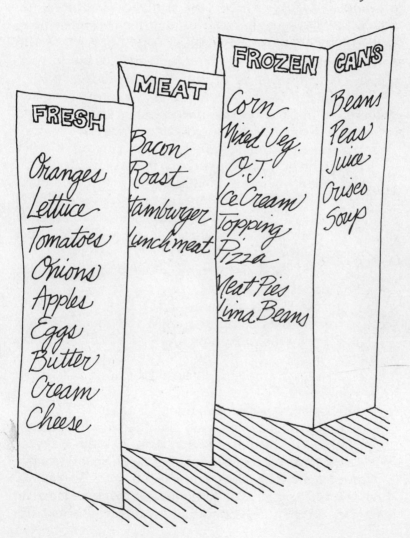

FRESH

Oranges
Lettuce
Tomatoes
Onions
Apples
Eggs
Butter
Cream
Cheese

MEAT

Bacon
Roast
Hamburger
Lunch meat

FROZEN

Corn
Mixed Veg.
O.J.
Ice Cream
Topping
Pizza
Meat Pies
Lima Beans

CANS

Beans
Peas
Juice
Crisco
Soup

weeks I shop heavily. The other weeks in the month I buy only perishable items. For a shopping list, I take a piece of 8½" x 11" paper, fold it into six columns (produce, meats, miscellaneous, utility, frozen, other—such as errands to the post office, etc.), and jot down what we need. I determine these needs from recipes as I make out our weekly menus, from things I observe during the day, and from the list in our food storage room, which indicates items that need replenishing. This list can be folded as I shop so it's not too conspicuous, it fits any market, and it enables me to shop quickly with little chance of forgetting a needed item.

Also on the weekly agendum is a thorough house-cleaning, in addition to the daily picking up, wiping off, vacuuming in traffic areas, and dusting. Once a week—usually on Saturday morning—our five daughters and I go to work about the house. We approach the task as one would eat an elephant—cut it up in little pieces and take regular bites. In other words, it would be completely overwhelming and exhausting to do all of the heavy cleaning in any one day. So we've worked out a system whereby we add a special project to the usual weekly duties. These are:

First week: Dust or vacuum baseboards and other dust-collecting ridges and ledges.

Second week: Vacuum upholstered furniture; dust mirrors, picture frames, lamp shades, and lighting fixtures.

Third week: Wash windows, if any or all of them need washing.

Fourth week: Scrub and polish a floor or clean a carpet as required.

Fifth week (when there is one): Reorganize a drawer or cupboard, or clean one out, such as kitchen drawers, which pick up crumbs and fingerprints.

Our most significant weekly activity is, of course, honoring the Sabbath. (See previous chapter.)

There are some monthly duties too, such as cleaning the range. Furnace filters should be replaced about this

often during cold months (I only do the reminding here—
my husband does the work).

Semiannual or seasonal tasks may include rearranging
clothing in closets, preparing clothes for school, potting
some of the flowers to be housed for winter, and setting
out plantings in the spring.

Once or twice a year an extra heavy house cleaning
may be required. Some women like to do this gradually
throughout the year; others still enjoy the pioneer approach of doing it in a big way a couple of times a year.
This is when walls and ceilings are washed, rooms are re-
painted, mattresses are vacuumed, and other such duties
are performed.

If this sounds like a lot of work, remember that it includes duties for an entire year. Fortunately, you only have
to conquer them a day at a time. And along the way, keep
your perspective by occasionally referring to a story like
the following:

### MY NIGHT AT THE MOVIES

"You'd better hurry up and change," my husband said the other night. "You haven't forgotten
that tonight's the night we're going to the movies,
have you?"

"Change?" I said slowly. "Oh, then I ought to
put on a fresh apron, shouldn't I? And I'll need another pair of hot mitts. I've got gravy on these."

"No, no, honey," my husband said. "We're going to the movies. You can take off your apron and
your hot mitts. You don't need an apron when you
go to the movies."

"Oh, okay," I said. "Listen, you bundle up the
dirty clothes and we can stop and buy detergent
on the way. I'll put the vacuum cleaner and ironing
basket in the car."

"No, honey," my husband said again. "You're

not supposed to do any housework when you go to the movies. We're just going to sit there and watch the screen, you know. No, don't take the broom."

I did tuck a dust cloth in my purse, though. And I got my little portable sewing machine in the back seat without his noticing it, so I had that with me, too. You can forget a lot about going to the movies in 18 years of marriage, I realize. But I was pretty sure I wasn't supposed to just goof off the whole time. I felt a lot better with the dust cloth and the sewing machine with me, at least.

We went out and got in the car, as soon as I was ready. I felt pretty nervous at first, the farther we got away from the kitchen stove. But of course that's natural.

I was as excited as a kid by the time we turned on to Route 96A. My husband says it was worth all the trouble, just to see my face when I saw the lights of Geneva. He pulled off to the side of the road and we looked across the water at the lights.

"Well, there's Geneva," my husband said. "And in 10 minutes we'll be driving up in front of Schine's Theater." He patted my knee. "You deserve it," was all he said, but I knew then that 18 years of raising children, keeping house, cooking and washing had not gone unnoticed.

I'll never forget what it was like, walking into that movie theater. And he was right about the sewing machine. He made me leave it in the car, and he was perfectly right; it was much too dark in there to sew.

I did dust the backs and arms of the seats around us, as many as I could reach, but I didn't do another thing, that whole two hours.

It was a once-in-a-lifetime experience, or pretty close to it, anyway, the way things seem to be going.

I squeezed my husband's hand, when at last we drove up in front of the house at the end of the evening. "I'll work harder than ever," I promised him. "You won't regret this." (Margaret Houser. Used with permission of the Gesell Institute.)

# 7
## *To Be A Helpmeet*

*"And the Lord God said,*
*It is not good*
*that the man should be alone;*
*I will make him*
*an help meet for him."*
*(Genesis 2:18)*

One day the telephone rang at our house and an irate voice demanded, "Are you the lady who wrote that book?"

I prepared to defend myself, gulped, and said, "Yes."

She hurried on, almost in a scream: "I just want to tell you that before you can run a perfect house, you've got to have a perfect husband. And when you get the answer to that, let me know!" With that, she banged the receiver down.

Needless to say, homemaking and child-rearing have to be a team effort on the part of husband and wife. Family living can be much more successful if the husband does his part too, and is cooperative and capable, helpful and happy. It takes one to spoil a marriage; it takes two to make a good one.

To me, the ideal marriage is where each partner does everything possible for the happiness of his spouse. If something matters to one, it should matter to the other. If the wife needs some shelves built or would like her husband to accompany her to visit an ailing friend, he should comply. If he asks for homemade bread or wants his collars starched, she should grant his wishes. Little things mean a lot and prepare the way for the big things.

A beautiful marriage is based on two people's desire to bring out the best in one another. They have entered marriage with preparations and expectations for success. It is said that the loveliest words Sir Winston Churchill ever penned were those of his wife, Clementine, so many years ago on the day they were married in St. Margaret's Church in London. In the church registry, on the day of his marriage, he wrote, "In September 1908 I married and lived happily ever after."

It is not the intent of this book to discuss a husband's responsibilities in providing for the spiritual, physical, emotional, and social welfare of his wife and family. Rather, let's discuss how the wife can best help him to fulfill these obligations, how she can most effectively work with him, as expressed in these lines by Henry Wadsworth Longfellow, from "The Song of Hiawatha":

> As unto the bow the cord is,
> So unto the man is woman,
> Though she bends him, she obeys him,
> Though she draws him, yet she follows,
> Useless each without the other!

I feel that it's essential for a wife to assist her husband in providing well for the family, not by going out and getting a job, but by remaining home and managing well. My neighbor commented the other day that she could stay home and save more money than she could go out and earn. This is true for most women, particularly if children are still at home.

I once read a clever magazine article about how to marry the man with the most money. The answer: learn to make the most of your man's money. In other words, be a smart consumer so your money will go as far as possible. Avoid waste (Brigham Young said that some women can throw more out the back door with a teaspoon than many men can bring in the front door with a wheelbarrow). Practice the "make-it-yourself" theory with everything from clothing to homemade bread. Cultivate a garden and can, freeze, or dry fruits and vegetables. Keep the mending up to date. Know how to remake and be creative with home furnishings so your house can be charming without being unnecessarily expensive. Work with your husband to prevent letting things around the home and yard become run down. If a piece of tile comes loose in the bathroom, fix it promptly before all the pieces around it fall off too. If a seam in the carpet is coming unstitched, mend it quickly before someone's toe snags it and tears up the carpet. If a slat in the fence falls out, encourage your husband to put it right back. Help him to look successful financially by how you and the children dress and by how you keep up your home. Never forget that looking attractive is more a matter of pride, ambition, and resourcefulness than it is of income.

My husband, Hank, says that one of the wisest things a woman can do to help her husband is to enthusiastically welcome him home at the close of his work day by looking attractive and refreshed and with the table set and dinner ready. He says that all the pressures of a man's day seem to melt away when he's greeted by a lovely wife, a good dinner, and a pleasant home environment. This type of setting can provide just the relief and relaxation he needs in order to prepare himself to once again face the competitive world on the morrow. In most cases, the better a wife fulfills her responsibilities in the home, the more motivated the husband is to do his part well.

But in spite of a man's best efforts, sometimes the income just does not cover the cost of living. There are ways a wife can supplement it without leaving the home or adding stress or pressure to family living. The time and energy some women expend in complaining and pitying themselves because of a lack of money could well be directed toward some profitable home-enterprise pursuits. Dressmaking, doing alterations for a clothing store, making uniforms and costumes, tending other people's children, conducting a preschool one afternoon a week, making candy or pastries or sandwiches for a nearby restaurant, freelance writing or artwork, bookkeeping or typing a few hours a week for a local business, giving music lessons, tutoring students, preparing handmade gifts for Christmas and other occasions—these are just a few of the opportunities available. The list could go on—just as long as there are talents and abilities.

A wife should work with her husband in putting their economic house in order. They should avoid overextending themselves, but instead, they should live within their means and build up a substantial reserve in savings. During times of plenty, they should heed the counsel of Church leaders and put away in their homes a storehouse of clothing and food.

Above all, a husband and wife should strive together to be worthy of the blessings and promises of the Lord in material matters as well as spiritual. It's very evident through his word that he wants us to be prosperous and that he promises us we will be so through our faithfulness. One of the many references to this is in 2 Nephi 1:20: "And he hath said that: Inasmuch as ye shall keep my commandments ye shall prosper in the land...."

Latter-day leaders of the Church echo this counsel and urge us to reflect the spirit of the gospel by being progressive and industrious, just as the Book of Mormon term "deseret" implies. Laziness, carelessness, and slothfulness have no part in the gospel plan. Furthermore, misdirected values and selfishness that take away from our families and homes that which they need are not in keeping with the gospel.

It should be remembered that prosperity cannot always be measured by income. Sometimes the Lord blesses and helps his faithful servants to prosper indirectly, such as through increased opportunities, additional advantages, extra strength and ambition, more positive attitudes, or fewer problems and expenses.

As husbands and wives, we must know the will of the Lord concerning those who keep his commandments, and then have faith in his promises and work to make them come true.

Someone said that Abraham Lincoln was great not because he was born in a log cabin, but because he was able to get out of it. In other words, the only virtue in being poor is in getting over it.

Of further importance in being a worthy helpmate is to truly be a lady. The more a woman looks or acts like a man, the less he likes her. Femininity is a priceless gift; it's tragic to see a woman lose it. She must work every day to preserve it; it's so easy to let it disappear a bit at a time. This reminds me of a man and woman who drove up to a theater, parked their automobile, and prepared to enter the building. By the time the man had approached the woman's side of the car, anticipating opening the door for her and helping her out, she was already getting out. He commented that he could be a gentleman if she would be a lady.

Sometimes a woman forgets who she is and becomes too independent and self-sufficient. In order to help her, she needs an occasional refresher course in the basic elements of femininity and charm. The modern woman knows, just as have all her sisters through the ages past, that there is only one way to bring out the best in a man. It's all in her charm.

What is charm? Margery Wilson calls it "the perfume of the soul." A more expanded definition is that a charming woman lets her husband know, through everything she says and does, how special he is. She is adoring, admiring, and appreciative. Even though she is a mature woman, she retains that ever-appealing quality of girlishness. She is spontaneous, responsive, and warm. She replaces moodiness and nagging, both of which her husband detests, with happiness and inspiration. She never forgets that a man will give all that he has for a woman's smile.

Paramount in her duties, a wife must help her husband honor his priesthood and magnify his related responsibilities.

She should be deeply grateful if her husband has brought the priesthood into their home. If not, she will fast and pray for this to happen. One latter-day prophet, in speaking to a group of women whose husbands were not active in the Church, told them that in many cases, if they were to live as though they had this blessing, it would eventually be theirs. He said that all too often a woman cries because her husband cannot take her to the temple, when in reality she isn't prepared to go either. She plans to give up her coffee as soon as he quits smoking. She intends to become active in the ward as soon as he's ready to attend meetings with her.

It is a blessed family where a faithful father declares, as did Joshua of old, "As for me and my house, we will serve the Lord."

But this won't actually happen to its fullest extent unless the wife, as the home manager, makes the plans and preparations and causes it to work. For instance, she will arrange mealtimes so her husband can call the family together for prayer. She will be on schedule on Mondays so refreshments are ready and everything is in order for family home evening. This includes directing the children in completing their homework and music practicing before dinner so they can be free afterwards for this special evening.

She sets the stage for a spiritual Sunday by performing her duties well on Saturday.

She sends her husband off to meetings with a full stomach and a light heart.

When his Church responsibilities are heavy, she endeavors not to add to his burden by complaining or criticizing.

She keeps confidences should she become aware of a confidential matter. She prays for discernment and wisdom in everything she says and does, so as not to detract from any position of leadership her husband may have.

She is gracious and helpful to ward and stake members

who call on the phone or come to the door, regardless of
the hour. She eagerly entertains people in her home, gladly
serves on committees, and devotedly holds any jobs asked
of her within the realm of her health and strength.

Regardless of how capable and efficient she may be,
though, this is all misdirected if she forgets her place—fails
to remember who she is—and takes over where her husband should preside. This would be in direct opposition
to the Lord's plan. There is order in all things pertaining
to the kingdom of God. Her husband is the presiding
officer; she is his "first counselor." He is the head of the
house; she is the heart of the home.

A woman should realize that one of the greatest blessings a father can bring to his family through his worthiness
and devotion is to draw close to the Holy Ghost so that
he can walk in the light of revelation for himself and for his
family. To know the will of the Lord concerning his family
would be the ultimate in spiritual gifts. A wife will help her
husband prepare himself for this counsel and will then
abide by it when it is received.

A visitor on Temple Square in Salt Lake City pointed to
the temple and exclaimed to the guide, "You mean to say
that a man can marry a woman in there and live with her
forever? You'd have to be either crazy or inspired."

The guide replied, "Really, neither is correct, though
we do hope for a degree of inspiration in selecting our
mates. We fast and pray and try to decide wisely as we
choose our eternal companions, but mostly it's a matter of
making our marriages work."

Yes, it does take a practically perfect husband (as well
as a practically perfect wife) to make a practically perfect
home. This probably won't happen the first year, maybe
not even during the first ten or twenty years. It may take a
lifetime. But it's the direction, not just the destination, that
counts.

# 8

## "Lead Me, Guide Me, Walk Beside Me"

*"A mother is not
a person to lean on, but rather
a person to make leaning unnecessary."
—Dorothy Canfield Fisher*

**A** registered nurse of many years' experience in the obstetrics ward of a hospital told a group of us mothers in a baby care demonstration, "Teach your baby an orderly way of life by (1) bathing him at the same time each day, either morning, afternoon, or evening (the time doesn't matter, but select one and stay with it; a bath is one of a baby's most dramatic events in the day, and he'll soon regulate all his activities from that point if it's consistent), and (2) feeding him no oftener than every three hours and no less frequently than every five hours (except at night)."

As he grows a little, parents can help him further to establish order in his life through good eating and sleeping habits. Regular meal times, nap times, and going-to-bed times usually result in healthy, happy children who are then free to enjoy play times and outings unencumbered by tears and tantrums. Structure in a few things leads to greater freedom in many things. And good habits of cleanliness and personal hygiene easily follow, if they are carefully taught.

Neatness, too, should become the child's way of life as he gradually learns during the first five years of his life to pick up his toys (with lots of help at first) before he goes on to the next activity, to put away his clothes as he takes them off, and to make his bed every morning as part of the dressing procedure (he needs a great deal of assistance here, too) before he starts to play or goes to school.

Simple tasks about the home and yard are another vital step in his progress. A good home should closely resemble an apprentice shop—a great laboratory for learning—where each child acquires valuable skills through working side by side, hand over hand, with his parents.

His duties should gradually become more complex as he matures, until he has learned the basic skills of living—everything from changing a tire for the boys to baking a beautiful pie for the girls.

Such responsibility gives the child something even more valuable than the skills; it also helps him develop self-mastery, self-ownership. If he gains mastery over little things, like making his bed every day, he can develop control over greater things, like himself.

Self-discipline is one of the greatest gifts you can help a child acquire. Then whatever his talents and abilities are, he'll be able to make the most of them. Without self-mastery, even the most richly endowed person usually wastes his abilities. Training your child early and consistently in this manner provides another bonus feature: you as his mother can gradually do less *for* him so you can do more *with* him. When he shares in the physical responsibility of his self and the home, you can then elevate your attention to creative, cultural, and spiritual levels.

Inseparably connected with helping children establish self-discipline through the development of good habits is the effective use of discipline whenever it's called for. Wise parents understand that discipline should be a learning experience, not just a punishment. Through punishment, a parent controls a child's action, but that's only part of the task. Through effective discipline, a parent can teach a child to control his own actions. Discipline assures him that his parents care about him and are helping protect him.

Two little girls were sitting on the steps of a porch when one of them was called home by her mother for dinner. The other one commented, "I wish my mother cared enough to call me home for dinner."

A young woman said that through her dating years her parents would never give her a time to be in at night. All they would say was, "We'll just leave it up to you. We're sure you will do what is best." She felt that that was more responsibility than she wanted, so she would often make up a time to tell her date just to make him think her parents cared. She said that all through those years she longed for more parental control. The fact that her parents left things entirely up to her judgment because, as they said, "You are such a good girl," made her feel almost unloved.

Actually, discipline is to a child like a fence is to a cow. Just as the animal noses its way along the fence to feel that it's there, so children have a natural urge to find the fence. They want to know that it's there; it gives them confidence, security, and protection.

As parents, we should not fence our child in too much, however. This might force him to jump the fence. We should endeavor rather to build the right fence for him so that he feels free to do what he should do. We should help him know that freedom means his right to choose the set of restrictions or laws under which he wants to live. Further, we should help him see that the only sets of laws that bring peace and joy are the laws of the land and the laws of the Lord.

We can learn effective techniques for discipline through Relief Society mother education classes and a careful selection of child guidance books. Thus, we can avoid the disastrous pitfalls of attempting to force the child rather than to control him; of colliding with him through a clash of wills rather than to sidestep the struggle for power; of losing our control in the effort to control him, thus reducing ourselves to screaming, nagging, threatening, insulting, or hitting parents. Remember, yelling at your children to get them to do something is like using the horn to stop your car going downhill!

In their very helpful book *Children: The Challenge* (Hawthorn, 1964), Dr. Rudolph Dreikurs and Vicki Soltz point out that one of the most effective ways to discipline a child is through application of the law of cause and effect. In other words, if a parent lets a child feel the effects or consequences of his own negative actions, he'll have a true learning experience and be headed toward self-control.

Life itself is full of consequences that teach children vital lessons quickly. The use of consequences eliminates much scolding, punishing, and nagging on the part of parents. As a result, rebellion and resentment are not built up within the child. A child has a keen sense of fair play. If the consequence is fair and what he deserves, he takes his medicine and seldom needs a second dose.

There are two types of consequences:

1. Natural, in which the parent stands back and lets life itself teach the child. For example, if a child doesn't come for dinner when he is called, he misses dinner and doesn't eat anything until breakfast.

2. Logical, in which there isn't a natural consequence or else it is dangerous, so a logical consequence is structured by the parents. For example, if a child starts to play in the street, he must come into the house. If he cannot handle his freedom to play outside without going into the street, then he loses his freedom.

Following are examples of consequences as they apply to teaching children to share in the responsibilities of the home. The same principles can be applied to temper tantrums, sassing, bedwetting, lying, stealing—and most other usual childhood problems.

1. If a child's dirty clothes are not put in the hamper or clothes chute, then the clothes cannot be washed by mother. He either wears soiled clothes or washes them himself.

2. If a child doesn't put away his toys, they may be placed on the "unwanted toy shelf" until he has missed them sufficiently to take better care of them.

3. If older children (or mothers or fathers!) leave articles of clothing or other belongings littered around,

these articles may be placed in a "mad bag." This is just a large grocery bag in which items are kept until they are redeemed with a nickel or dime by the owner. The money, of course, goes to the person who had to pick up the items to compensate him or her for the "undue maid service" rendered. Or if the owner of the neglected items is low on cash, he may redeem his things by performing some special service for the person who had to pick up after him. Once in awhile it might be necessary to declare a "mad bag emptying day" in which no one leaves the house until all of his articles have been redeemed.

A correlation to this idea appeared in a local newspaper. A family spent a few days at a campground in a neighboring state. When they returned home, they received a note from the proprietor of the campground saying that they had left some personal belongings behind that were being mailed to them C.O.D. The belongings arrived—a collection of empty pop bottles and cans and other assorted trash—for which they had to pay thirty-six dollars in mailing charges!

4. When children balk at doing the dishes, unless the reason is legitimate, the consequence is that anyone who is "too tired" or "too busy" to do the dishes is also "too tired" or "too busy" to receive any phone calls or watch television that evening or enjoy any other privileges, and must spend his time resting in his room with lights out and radio off.

5. Being aroused from bed for a trip to the garage may be required for the boy who leaves his bike out or who forgets to set out the garbage cans.

6. If a child carelessly loses or breaks something, he must replace the item with his own money, or at least make a substantial contribution, according to his age, toward its replacement.

7. If a child leaves home in the morning without making his bed and putting his room in order, he may be called

home from school or wherever he is to do his chores. (What's a lesson in arithmetic if he cannot handle basic responsibility? And one such experience provides a life-long lesson!) I once received the following note from a schoolteacher:

Dear Mrs. Hoole: Recently you conducted a home-making seminar in our city. Last week two mothers came to my class to take their children home to complete some unfinished duties. I just want you to know that as a schoolteacher I appreciate this. When parents insist that responsibilities be carried out at home, it makes it a lot easier for us at school.

8. A toddler spilled his milk and food at every meal, and his mother would talk to him and scold him as she crawled around on the floor cleaning up the mess. Finally it occurred to her that the child was enjoying the floor show! When she realized that no hungry child plays with his food, she quickly removed him from the high chair when he started to play, and the spilling ceased.

9. If parents return home after an evening out and find the house in shambles when the children have been instructed to tidy up, being awakened at a late hour to do so helps them remember evermore to follow such instructions.

10. If the family is out driving and the children are fussing and arguing about sitting by the windows, father can turn the car around, take them home, and have each child sit by a window of the house for an hour.

Even though some of these approaches to discipline may seem drastic, they are not harsh or cruel—and they can be effective.

Because it's difficult to think creatively during a moment of crisis, a wise parent will plan in advance what consequences might be used to fit a certain situation. In other words, it might be well to make a list of typical family problems and then take time to think through what consequences might apply. Then when the next problem arises, the parent, instead of desperately resorting to yelling, threatening, or punishing, will be prepared to discipline the child effectively, and a true learning experience will be had by the child.

This method also helps a parent avoid a power clash with a child. It is impossible and wrong to force a child to do something, and if a parent attempts to do this, he'll probably reduce himself to a desperate, yelling ogre, accomplishing nothing, but undermining both his and his child's self-respect. Even though a parent cannot *force* a child, he can determine what he is going to do and in that way *control* the child. For example, a parent cannot, without being a brute, make a child do a certain task, but he can forbid the child to leave the house until the task is done. And if the child tries to stall, he can be grounded an hour for every five minutes of stalling.

Another example: If the children are fighting over which television program to watch, instead of a parent's trying to solve the problem for them and thereby joining the fight, he can merely turn off the set and say, "When you have solved your problem, you may turn the TV back on." Within seconds the children will have made the decision and will be happily and quietly watching TV.

Another example: If a child's crying annoys you, don't try to stop it. Merely leave the room or take the child to his own room. He'll soon stop crying, because it's no fun to put on a show without an audience.

When a child is made to feel responsible for his own self and his own affairs, he gains in maturity and the parent is free from annoying problems that he shouldn't try to solve anyway. For instance, a little girl came running home to mother with the complaint that children were throwing sticks at her. The mother said, "Well, come into the house if it bothers you."

The child quickly responded, "Oh, no, it doesn't," and

she happily ran back to play.

A pediatrician who spoke to a group of parents at a fireside said that almost everything a child does is for a pay-off, for some type of attention. Parents must be careful that they don't pay off a child unintentionally and thus cause him to repeat an undesirable act. For example, a punishment can be a pay-off to a child. He would rather be scolded than ignored, so he does something naughty to get attention, even though it's negative attention. Generally speaking, the cardinal rule of raising children is: *Applaud a child's positive behavior, and ignore (as far as possible) his negative actions.*

Spanking a child is usually a sign of bankruptcy on the part of parents—they're out of ideas and feel desperate and frustrated. But if we do resort to spanking, we should do it in a mature way, maintaining our dignity and control through turning the child on end and spanking him soundly, not hitting at him harshly. Someone has said,

> When raising a child by the book,
> You can—if sufficiently vexed—
> Hasten the results by applying the book
> As well as applying the text.

Dr. Fitzhugh Dodson, author of the book *How to Parent* (Freeport, New York: Nash Publishing Corporation, 1970), says, "We've unconsciously assumed that if we raise a child to be happy and well-adjusted, he will be moral and ethical too. But it's not necessarily so." We must teach him that honesty is the only policy, not just the best policy. Careful instruction along the lines of the Ten Commandments should be an integral part of his upbringing. "A few headaches now can save us from heartaches later on." (Richard L. Evans.)

Above all, we as parents must realize that if we are to give our children good habits, we must have good habits ourselves. If they are to learn maturity and self-control from us, we must also grow in these areas. A healthy adjustment to life on our part becomes the pattern for their adjustment.

### CHILDREN LEARN WHAT THEY LIVE

*If a child lives with criticism,*
  *He learns to condemn.*
*If a child lives with hostility,*
  *He learns to fight.*
*If a child lives with ridicule,*
  *He learns to be shy.*
*If a child lives with jealousy,*
  *He learns to feel guilty.*
*If a child lives with tolerance,*
  *He learns to be patient.*
*If a child lives with encouragement,*
  *He learns confidence.*
*If a child lives with praise,*
  *He learns to appreciate.*
*If a child lives with fairness,*
  *He learns justice.*
*If a child lives with security,*
  *He learns to have faith.*
*If a child lives with approval,*
  *He learns to like himself.*
*If a child lives with acceptance and friendship,*
  *He learns to find love in the world.*

  —*Dorothy Law Nolte*

In teaching a child respect—first of things and then of people and ideals—we too must be respectful of him, his things, and what is important to him. We should be mindful that the terms and tones of our conversation always denote sincere respect. We should save our "fire alarm" voice for when there really is a fire.

In connection with this, we should talk to him in posi-

tive, complimentary terms. Insulting him and picking at him
is never in order. When he stumbles while walking along a
path, we might respond, "Are you all right? I hope you
didn't hurt yourself too much. I know how you feel—I've
stumbled like that before too." We should avoid such
phrases as "Can't you watch where you're going?"

We should be careful to say, "Here, let me help you stir
that," rather than "Don't stir that. You always spill." We
should say, "I want to see how nice your room looks before
you leave for school" instead of "Don't you go to school
until your room is in order."

And when we fail in using effective techniques and lose
our self-control, he must hear our admission and apology.
It takes a big person to apologize. This in itself can be another good lesson to him. It's been well stated that in case
of conflict, the nicest person will apologize first. We don't
have to be perfect to be parents—just honest.

Parents hope to prepare each of their children to be-
have properly in public places, such as stores, the homes of
others, and church. As an example, let's discuss the challenge of taking him to church. Before entering the chapel,
we might take him to the fountain for a drink of water and
then to the bathroom, and help him understand that that
has to last until after the meeting. We should make it a
point to be a few minutes early so we can get comfortably
settled and thus avoid a scramble as the meeting starts.
We should have already practiced at home how to sit
quietly in a chapel. Should the child misbehave, he should
find it more unpleasant to be taken out of the meeting than
to remain. By this, we mean that he should not be allowed
to run and play in the halls; rather, he should be taken to
a classroom and firmly, but kindly, taught to sit quietly.
Then he should be praised generously for learning to be
reverent.

Still speaking as one set of parents to another, may we
now build upon the foundation described in the foregoing

and share some ideas about developing and enjoying children.

First, we should love our children and listen to them.

Numerous helpful books have been written on child guidance; but if you haven't read any of these books, or even if you've broken many of the rules they suggest, your children will probably turn out well if you do two things: *love* them and *listen* to them.

Let's talk first about love. Although it is possible to indulge and overprotect our children, it is impossible to give them too much real love. Even when it is necessary for us to reprimand a child, he should understand that we do so out of love for him and are in no way rejecting him. Actually, children need love most when they seem to deserve it least!

As a parent, we should not only love our child—he must *feel* that love. It's the response that the love causes within that really counts. To help a child feel the love he needs, it's good to remember that a parent's love should comprise seven qualities, each of which begins with the letter "A." Let's briefly discuss each one.

1. *Attention*

Children demand attention constantly in one way or another. We're going to have to give it to them anyway, so why not give them the very best attention possible? We should make the time we spend with them really count for good fun and meaningful experiences.

2. *Availability*

Actually, this is more of an attitude than an act. Not only should we make a point to be present when our children need us, but our children must have the distinct feeling that their welfare and happiness are of great importance to us, and that we're glad to be truly available to them.

3. *Acceptance*

Unless our child feels our unqualified acceptance—

whether he hates the piano or excels in baseball or is a top student or not—he won't gain the maximum benefits of our love. A mother must realize that she is not to mold each child into what she considers to be an ideal person; rather, she should help him and guide him in becoming the best of whatever he is. Naturally, some traits, such as dishonesty, cannot be tolerated in anyone, but the world is desperately in need of people with varied contributions to make. Just as a garden is made more beautiful with a variety of flowers, so is this world made better because of the differences of the individual people in it.

4. *Approval*

Children thrive on approval or encouragement and wither with criticism. Some parents think they are training their children if they criticize them often, but discipline and training should be positive actions, not negative. Psychologists say that an encouraged child is a happy, well-adjusted child; a discouraged child is unhappy and is often naughty or poorly adjusted.

5. *Appreciation*

Appreciation is closely linked to acceptance and approval, but it's vital enough to the well-being of a child to merit individual mention. We should help him know that he's appreciated by showing him and telling him. And we shouldn't just tell him—sometimes we can also write to him. A special thank-you note from us would be treasured by him. At "Back-to-School Night" a mother left a note of appreciation in the desks for each of her children. The children were delighted when they found the notes the next day, and they tried even harder to do their best work.

6. *Advantages*

If we really love our children, we'll give them every possible advantage. We'll give them the advantage of learning right from wrong and of establishing a sound value system. We'll give them the advantage of learning to work hard and thoroughly. We'll give them the advantage of learning to get along well with their fellowmen. We'll give them the advantage of knowing the feeling of earning money for an honest hour's labor. We'll give them the advantage of making, doing, and acting, not just of having, watching, and reacting. Two little boys built a toy car. When it was almost finished, one of them asked the other, "Which do you think is the most fun, making or having?" The other replied, after a thoughtful moment, "Making." Let's give our children real advantages—the ones of lasting value.

7. *Affection*

In our own natural way, we demonstrate our love for our children through affection. It's been found that infants who are denied affection during the early weeks of their lives often grow up with impaired personalities. Affection helps a child blossom as does sunshine a flower.

That's a brief summation of seven qualities that make the love children need. Now let's discuss *listening*.

Wise parents learn, sometimes the hard way, to listen much more and talk much less. Teenagers whose parents really listen to them feel understood. Children of all ages need to be heard out, to be listened to. Have you ever heard a child of about four say, "Don't say 'no' until I say to," or "Mommy, listen with your eyes too"?

Not only is listening actively a matter of courtesy and good personal relations, but it can also be a clue to what the child is thinking about and where he's been and what he's doing. A wise parent will also listen "between the lines," and hear the sighs, heart throbs, and unspoken words.

To be really effective listeners, we should understand and practice four typical listening responses.

The first is the *advice-giving* response, in which we offer our opinion. This type of response is all right in matters such as when a child asks what dress to wear. It's not the best response, however, when he announces that he's failing algebra. Simply telling him that he should study harder may make us feel better, but it probably won't help him.

The second response is the *evaluating* or *judging* one. There are times when quick judgment on our part is appropriate, but when a child says, "I hate school," a response such as "You shouldn't feel that way" is hardly helpful. In such an instance, we might use the third response, which is *probing*. Through a series of questions, we learn why he hates school. Only then does he feel that we understand him and are in a position to help.

The fourth response is *understanding,* when we reflect back to the child his feelings. This is the most difficult response, but it is often the most effective one, particularly when the matter is an emotional one. For instance, a child might ask, "Why can't we have a cabin in the mountains? All my friends' families have cabins." It would be unwise for us to use the advice-giving response and say, "Because cabins are too expensive, that's why," or to use the judging response and say, "Now you know that all your friends don't have cabins. Stop that exaggerating."

It would be better to probe: "Why would you like to have a cabin?" But to really understand him and let him feel understood, we should reflect back to him his feelings, such as, "You really would like a family cabin, wouldn't you." Instead of feeling squelched and rejected, he suddenly feels understood and opens up a bit more: "Yes, then we could do lots of fun things together as a family." Then we reflect with him a bit more. "You enjoy doing things with the family, don't you." After a series of exchanges such as these, we realize that it's not the cabin but more time with the family that the child really wants. And he has the satisfaction of knowing that his feelings have been seriously considered and that he has been completely understood. The way is also prepared for further effective communication between him and us.

As a bonus feature, listening can also be delightfully entertaining. Children are such fun! Five-year-old Becky said, "Don't bother me. I'm thinking my dreams." Another little girl expressed it well when she sipped her first ginger ale and remarked, "Ginger ale tasted like my foot feels when it goes to sleep."

Our family was camping one summer. After enjoying the program at the lodge during the evening, we climbed partway up the mountain to our tents. Just as we were getting settled in the cots, two-year-old Gregory said, "I'm thirsty." It was pitch-black outside, and the closest water was half a mile away, so mother tried everything to talk him out of a drink until morning. But he persisted, as only two-year-olds can, in his demand for water. The problem was finally solved when three-year-old Spencer spoke up: "Oh, Gregory, just make a bubble and then swallow it!"

Yes, we must love our children and listen to them. There's no better advice for child-rearing.

A little boy once asked, "Mama, why is it that you love me more in the morning than you do at night?" Any mother of a normal, noisy, active child will readily understand such a question. No matter how good one's intentions are to be a loving mother *all* day long, by evening nerves are a little frazzled, one's patience has worn a bit thin, and one is often more than eager to put the children to bed.

How about helping your little ones to feel loved all day long by taking out some "love insurance" for the evening. After toys are picked up, clothes are put away, and pajamas are on, take a few extra minutes for a special quiet time. Gather your little ones around you and read a story, sing a song, or chant a nursery rhyme or finger play, and then visit for a few minutes with each child. This may sound difficult at first, but the chances are good that you'll find the children so cooperative and eager as they anticipate this special time that the whole thing will take less time than getting them to bed took before.

You may well discover that the crowning point of this

quiet time is a private visit with each child at his bedside. (If another child interrupts the visit, he loses his visit that night. Such a thing rarely has to happen, however.) Busy children don't usually take time during the day to really talk to parents, but at bedtime, when they're glad to postpone sleep for a few minutes, they're extremely eager to talk. This is the time for parents to listen and listen. Many precious experiences of the day are shared; and feelings, both distressing and delightful, are aired and true communication between parent and child may be enjoyed.

Such visits may even produce some timely confessions. Once as I was about to leave our son's bedside, he decided to tell me that under his bed were bananas, milk, and cereal, all ready for a midnight snack. The result? He enjoyed his snack in the kitchen with a clear conscience.

You might make it traditional to ask each child to relate his happiest experience of the day. Exercising a bit of hindsight is good for anyone, and this will help the child live the day fully in order to relate a happy experience, and he will tend to repeat the happy experience. After an especially fun and exciting Fourth of July, our little three-year-old said, "This has been such fun. Let's do this day again."

A bedtime visit—even older children love such an occasion—can often be the key to the door of communication with a child. Now, if you have one or two children, such a routine can be fairly simple. But if yours is a large family, you may have to be ingenious to work it in. Perhaps you can have a quiet time and visit with some of the children (all of the boys, for instance) one evening, and then all the other children (the girls) may enjoy their special time the next night. Better yet, how about Dad making the rounds with Mother or taking turns with her. The children will be delighted to have Daddy do this, and it's very likely he will enjoy it too!

This will take a little time, but it could well be the most

important activity of your day as far as your children are concerned. Often when a child calls repeatedly for a drink of water after having been put to bed, it's not water but mother or dad that he wants. This special gift of your undivided attention will give an island of security to sleep on and a meaningful experience on which he can build the next day.

Be sure to take out some love insurance for your children, according to the age and temperament of the child. This is certain to pay countless dividends.

As a mother, I consider myself a harbor—available for pleasant association in calms or protection during a storm. Whatever, my child should find peace and comfort through me in the home. In order to be this harbor, I must earnestly strive to be home as the children get up in the morning, come home from play or school, or after dates.

A high school girl who had been awarded a special scholarship was asked by a news reporter what she wanted to be. She answered, "I want to be an 'at home' mother." When he asked her to explain what she meant, she replied, "My mother worked all my life except for a two-week period when illness in our family caused her to stay home. It was during those two weeks that I decided I was going to be an 'at home' mother."

As parents, we need to be alert to every teaching moment. Casual comments, on-the-spot explanations, lessons when life itself is providing the visual materials are some of the best teaching opportunities.

Consciously "validating" each child every day is a must in rearing our children. Taking a little liberty with the dictionary's definition of "validate," we should regularly say or do something to enhance the child's self-worth. Encouraging him, praising something he has done, passing on a compliment heard about him, letting him have a success experience—these are some of the things we can do to validate our children.

We should realize the importance of helping the child to be socially well adjusted. Psychologists and sociologists rank this as number one in a child's development. He must like other people and others must like him. We should allow him broad experience in constructive play with other children and brothers and sisters. Learning to play well at five years of age means he's on the way to living well at fifteen and at fifty.

We should be cognizant of the tremendous influence friends and peer groups are to have in his life. We want him to have good friends. We can help him in this by striving to give him a healthy feeling of self-esteem, for we understand that the type of friends he selects will likely be a reflection of how he regards himself. In other words, a child who has healthy self-esteem will usually choose friends of high caliber. Furthermore, we will be gracious and courteous to his friends and make them feel welcome and comfortable in our home. We will gladly feed and entertain them, knowing that such is a small price to pay for all that may be gained through having our home a gathering place.

Along with serving meals at the dinner table that are planned to nourish his body, we will present conversation designed to enrich his spirit. The dinner hour is an ideal time to share a story or take turns reading aloud from a choice book. (Above all, we should avoid turning dinner into a setting for family battles. Problems and negative reports should be discussed privately at another time.)

Once a week we might eat in the dining room instead of the kitchen. (If you don't have a formal dining room, you could at least create a similar atmosphere in the kitchen with special table service and a centerpiece.) Along with just enjoying such an occasion, we could use this opportunity to teach children such things as how to use a butter knife, what the salad fork is for, and how to act when "out to dinner."

We should teach our child to streamline his life—to live

above either physical or mental clutter. We should help him to throw most things away after they have fulfilled their usefulness, but not to throw everything away. We need to guide him in the use of a personal treasure chest for those things that will have real meaning in his life.

We should take a great deal of time for family fun in and around the home, outings, vacations, doing many things together. We must build traditions and stress projects that add to family cohesiveness. We once spent six family home evenings making a family flag (more technically, a family gonfalon). As it hangs in a hallway of our home, the motto embroidered on it and the symbolism it depicts serve as reminders of who and what we are and where we hope to go.

Doing things together, on both a planned and a spontaneous basis, would be a major part of our family living. In other words, we would put great emphasis on making moments to remember.

As father and mother, we should strive to give our child the time and means whereby he can develop himself: arts and crafts supplies, musical instruments and lessons, sewing machine and fabrics, recipes and use of the kitchen, work bench and tools, papers, pencils, and desks, good books and cozy corners, balls, bats, and bikes. Just for fun, we could paint a hopscotch figure on the cement, either in the basement or outside. We might make an indoor swing from a large-size tire by inverting it and cutting it out.

We should teach our son to honor the priesthood and our daughter to respect it and live to share in its blessings.

### THE GIFT

There was a mother, and God sent her a boy baby. And the mother loved her baby. She loved his sparkling eyes and his clinging fingers. She loved the tininess of him and at the same time the greatness of him, for she knew that in him there was a man.

And the mother thought, "What gift can I give this child to prove my love for him?" And as she pondered it in her mind, she thought, "I will lay up money for him. I shall spend meagerly and save with diligence that he may have wealth to buy whatsoever his heart desires." And she held her child close, already proud of the gift she would give him.

But the next day as she stood looking into the crib of her sleeping baby, she thought, "No, money is not the greatest gift I can give him. I shall give him learning. The best books and the most renowned teachers in all the land shall be his."

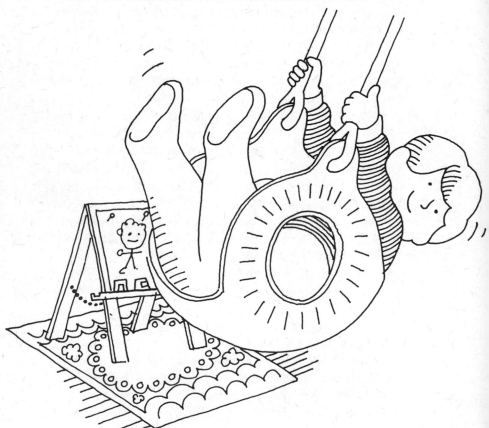

But in the stillness of the night when the distant stars lit the heavens and the whisperings of God could be heard, the mother knew that learning was not the greatest gift she could give her little one. There came to her the knowledge that the greatest gift she could bestow was a desire to love and to hold the priesthood of God, so she resolved in her heart that this should be her gift to him.

And so the child grew, and as he grew the mother taught him many things—and little by little she gave him the gift, for she also taught him of the goodness of God and his wondrous power.

And once, when the child was ill and the fever burned in his cheeks and parched his lips, she sought out the elders, and they came and laid their hands upon the child's head and blessed him. And when the sickness ebbed from the child and he marveled, she said, "It was God who made you well through the power of the priesthood. When you are twelve you may receive the priesthood, and when you are older, you may lay *your* hands upon the heads of the sick and bless them and heal them." And the child smiled, for it was a good and a great thing that was to come to him.

And when with chubby fingers the child partook of the Sacrament, watching the deacons with awe and a little envy as they went about their duties, the mother said, "When you are twelve, you may become a deacon and pass the Sacrament. This is the first calling in the priesthood of God." And the child watched earnestly and waited with longing for the day to arrive.

And time passed, and at length the day came, the day when the boy child was *twelve*. And on that day he received the gift, the gift of the priesthood, the power to act for God on earth, and the gift was of more worth than the vast treasures of King Solomon—more shining than the sun. And there was a light in the boy's eyes and a gladness in the mother's heart.

But as the child grew in body and in learning, so had the mother grown in wisdom and understanding, and she realized that although the gift had been given, now she must teach the child to honor and magnify it that it might be his forever.

So on Sabbath mornings when the softness of his bed coaxed the boy to stay, the mother with gentle kindness and great love roused him and sent him on his way.

And when he was asked by the elders to perform those duties in keeping with the gift, the mother urged him and guided him toward their accomplishment.

And when the gift began to be hidden in the clutter of many things, the mother brought it out again for the maturing boy to see, and it stayed precious in his sight, and the mother rejoiced—rejoiced that in the stillness of the night she had heard the whisperings of God. (Thelma J. Harrison, "The Gift," *Improvement Era*, January 1958.)

As parents, we should direct our best and most consistent efforts toward teaching our child to love and live the gospel of Jesus Christ. We would hope to accomplish this by first of all building and maintaining a good relationship with him—keeping the climate right.

Recent research has shown that there is a surprisingly low relationship between the religious sympathies of parents and their offspring. The degree to which children follow in the religious (or non-religious) footsteps of their parents appears to be most significantly related to the type and quality of relationship existing between parents and offspring, not merely upon how religious or righteous the parents are. (Victor B. Cline, "Obedience and Love," *Instructor*, June 1964.)

Next, we should endeavor to be models worthy of emulation. Inconsistency, compromise, and confusion should have no part in our living gospel standards. We should want him to follow us in every way.

*And again, inasmuch as parents have children in Zion, or in any of her stakes which are organized, that teach them not to understand the doctrine of repentance, faith in Christ the Son of the living God, and of baptism and the gift of the Holy Ghost by the laying on of the hands, when eight years old, the sin be upon the heads of the parents. (D&C 68:25.)*

We should make daily family prayers, weekly family home evenings, and proper observance of the Sabbath the means of teaching our children to know Jesus Christ and of sharing with them the doctrines of the Church and our testimonies of their truth and divinity.

We should set as our great goal exaltation as a family in the celestial kingdom. We should evaluate every thought and act according to whether it is bringing us closer to that realization.

We should humbly and prayerfully realize that none of this is a guarantee that the child will respond just as we would desire. Fortunately, most children do. There is always a chance, however, that a child, as a free agent and through many other influences upon him, will deviate from eternal family goals. If such a thing should happen, the only way to peace as a parent is to know that, according to the knowledge we had, we did our very best.

The mother of a wayward daughter referred to President David O. McKay's statement, "No other success can compensate for failure in the home," and asked, "When has a parent failed?"

The answer: "When he or she has given up."

We should ever teach and hope and pray that each child will find and follow the path that leads to eternal joy.

*Plastic little children made of heaven's clay,*
*Oh, Father, give us vision to mold them right this day.*
*Potential gods in miniature, we must have help from thee,*
*For how they're fashioned here today will endure*
*        throughout eternity.*

*—Author unknown*

# 9
## What Then?

*"Grandchildren are God's way
of compensating us
for growing old."*
—Anonymous

**M**arie, our devoted housekeeper in the mission home, was shedding tears in the mop bucket as she worked one day. When I inquired as to her problem, she broke into sobs and cried, "It's the fingerprints—I'm going to miss them so terribly."

After nearly four and a half years in Holland, my father had been released as mission president and our family was returning to Salt Lake City. The mission president called to succeed him had no children to make fingerprints.

At the time it was difficult for me, a girl of twenty-two, to really appreciate how anyone could ever feel bad about a lack of fingerprints. But now I understand.

The other day I mentioned to my sister, Donette, that I'll be a basket case the day we send the last child off to school. She responded, with insight, "Only temporarily, I'm sure. You'll be okay after the first fifteen minutes."

And so it must be. Accepting changes and adjusting to them are vital parts of life. The story is told about one of our General Authorities who called a man to preside over a stake. After counseling about leading the stake effectively, he added, "And start today to prepare for your release."

Fortunately, we'll never be released as mothers and fathers. That's why those callings are number one in importance. But the time does come when we're greatly relieved of much of the responsibility. What then? A wise woman will prepare a little all through the years for this change.

A neighbor once remarked to me how essential it is to "stay alive" during one's child-rearing years. As involved as a mother can be in caring for little mouths and bottoms the clock around, she must do as much as possible to avoid any rust or deterioration in her talents, interests, and abilities. This keeps the door open for purposeful living all one's life. Wilferd A. Peterson said, "You do not grow old, you become old by not growing.

As your family gradually needs you less and less, you can do more and more for yourself and others. Hopefully you won't get caught up in trivia and let the "thick of many thin things" become your way of life. Rather, you'll use this time for greater self-development and more meaningful service to others. You will strive to become a deeper person, one of more substance and quality.

It has been said that the quality of one's character can be determined by what one does when he doesn't have to do anything. I feel a great deal of respect for retired people who are engaged in such pursuits as furthering their education, either by returning to school or studying at home; who are enjoying some traveling; who are involved in service in their wards, stakes, and communities; and who find genealogical research and temple work an important part of their lives.

Above all, these should be the golden years of a marriage. Doing many more things together as husband and wife, growing in even greater love, and increasing in appreciation and companionship should highlight this chapter of your lives. Every minute of this togetherness should be treasured, knowing that it could come to a temporary end at any time.

I would enjoy being of service and assistance to our married children. I would like to help when babies are born, when a mother is ill, or when parents go out of town. It would please me to work with my daughters and daughters-in-law in home canning, quilting, and other such projects. I would invite their companionship and seek ways to be close to them.

Another worthy project at this juncture in life would be that of being a wonderful grandmother. I assume this to be a delightful role—the joys of children without the jobs! As one grandfather put it, "I love to have the grandchildren come and I love to have them go." A writer has said, "Grandchildren are God's way of compensating us for growing old." Even though many modern grandmothers don't match the lovable stereotype (you know, the sweet little old lady with her knitting, sitting in a rocking chair), their unique contribution to the lives of grandchildren remains the same.

> *My grandma is one of my best friends.*
> *She helped me build a rocket!*
> *She listens when I talk to her*
> *And gives me candies from her pocket.*
>
> *She tells me about the olden days*
> *And things that were happening then.*
> *I love her so that when we play games*
> *I sometimes let her win!*
>
> *—Mary Ellen Jolley*

It's a blessing for everyone concerned when grandmother (and grandfather, too) has the physical and emotional health to really enjoy grandchildren and knows what to do to become part of their lives and let them enjoy her. This is beautifully illustrated in the following story, written by the grandmother of my own children, my mother:

### From the Heart of a China Doll
### By Ada S. Van Dam

My name is Mary, and I am a china doll. A tiny, tiny china doll—about three inches tall and weighing just an ounce or so. The important part I have played in a couple of lives is out of all proportion to my size, because I have had a significant influence in several ways. I am now over sixty years old, but I still look as good as new because I have been given tender, loving care all these years. I have movable arms and legs that are fastened to my body with wires. Dainty slippers and stockings are painted on my tiny feet. My eyes are bright and sparkling. My brown hair is painted on my head in soft curls that are made for caressing. Everyone tells me that I have a very pretty face. I was given to a little girl with the nice, old-fashioned name of Ada when she was seven years old. She was delighted with me and gave me a warm welcome. It was she who gave me the name of Mary—one of the sweetest of all girl names.

Ada prepared a sturdy little cardboard box for my bed. I can still see the printing on the lid of that box: "Clinton's Safety Pins." She made some bedding for the little box so that I would be snug and warm. I found I liked it best when I was cozy and comfortable. My favorite coverlet was made from a small piece of bathrobe flannel and was blanket-stitched around the edges by Ada. And you should see my wardrobe! It was styled and handcrafted by Ada. She measured so carefully and then cut out her own paper patterns. The fabrics were scraps from family sewing. The tiny stitches showed fine workmanship for those little seven-year-old fingers. The seams were finished well for strength and neatness. There were hems, snaps, and buttons. There was a gray crepe-de-chine dress with tiny colored beads sewn in a fancy design; there was a golden-brown silk dress with a wee lace collar; there was a pair of rompers, also made from pretty silk. I observed that rompers were the proper attire for children of fifty years ago. Another dress that I was so proud to wear was of white poplin material. It had a set-in yoke, and oh, it was so pretty! These dresses were only a couple of inches long, you know, and I know that every stitch was done with love.

A doll is a favorite playmate of most girls. All the secrets of its owner are poured into its ears. As for Ada and me, sometimes she didn't even have to talk in order for me to know the things that were in her heart. As she played with me, making dresses, playing house, and even just daydreaming, she would always pretend that I was her own little girl—and I knew that her visions of the future and her heartfelt desires were that someday she would have little children of her own—real, breathing, talking children, sent from our Father in heaven to bless her home. And her thoughts went on and on through the years to the time when she would have her very own grandchildren and great-grandchildren. That is a woman's whole existence, the purpose for which she was created. How do I know all this? Well, I was there, you see, and I knew every wish that was in her heart. I was watching and listening from my Clinton's Safety Pins box-bed, while I was tucked under the coverlet that kept me warm.

And so the years came and went, and Ada grew up and married a fine man. She was blessed in having wonderful children to bring joy to her throughout eternity. And the plans she made for them, as well as for the grandchildren who would someday gladden her heart, were thought out in the greatest of detail. These were busy years, so I waited in my box, being played with only on special family occasions.

The day came when her very first grandchild turned seven. Ada was fifty, and she remembered the joy that I, her little china doll, had brought into her life on her own seventh birthday. Nothing would be more appropriate, she thought, than to give me

—her treasured china doll Mary—to this sweet little girl. You were that little granddaughter, Jean, and I well remember the day that I was taken to your home. Since that day I have proudly been kept among your keepsakes and you and I have shared many things together. Of course, I have been taken to school on "show and tell" days, and I have been the heroine on other occasions. It's been fun to have been a part of special times and to have seen and heard the family events. Yes, Jean, I have watched and listened with great interest. I'm just a doll, but if I could ever be a real person, I think I'd like to be a grandmother.

I'll never, just never, forget the giggling and fun time of "Toast is up!" With a kitchen full of grandchildren, Grandmother Ada would say, "Let's get ready." She would slip the slices of bread into the toaster, push the lever, and then stand in a certain corner of the kitchen, with her hands clenched tight. Even the little grandchild in the high chair would clench tiny fists. Everyone feigned excitement as they listened to the tick-tock of the toaster thermostat. As the toast popped up, Grandma Ada and all the clenched hands would be opened wide and arms would be thrown upward as everyone would laugh at this fun game. It was a "must" for every lunch time together.

"Cracker time!" was another grandmother-grandchildren fun time. As the cousins played in the swing set or the sandpile or hopscotched in Grandmother Ada's backyard, a certain heart-warming ritual took place at midmorning. I guess grandmothers always know that grandchildren like snack time, so a goodly supply of soda crackers was placed on the tray. She would greet you with "Cracker time!" and all the youngsters would come scampering from every corner of the yard. I was often tempted to try eating a soda cracker myself so that I could be a part of this wonderful grandmother-grandchildren experience.

And, Jean, do you remember the day Grandma taught you to ride the bicycle? Oh, what a day! You were just a very little girl. Your friends rode their bicycles "clear around the block" and you couldn't even balance yours. You wanted to learn so much. You couldn't wait until Daddy came home from work to help you, and Mommy was expecting a new baby. You wanted some help with that bike, so you asked Grandma if she would help. And she did! As I said before, "Oh, what a day!" She helped you get on the bicycle, gave you a push, and ran alongside to balance you. You'd fall, and then the two of you would do it again. And again. And again. You would coax to wait until tomorrow, but Grandmother Ada wouldn't listen. You would say, "I'll break my new bicycle when I fall over." Grandma would say, "We'll get it fixed. Never mind." You would say, "I hurt myself." She would say, "I can't see any blood." And do you know what? Before that "Oh, what a day!" was over, you were riding from corner to corner and loving every minute of it. When Grandmother took you and the bicycle home, you called all the family to come out on the sidewalk, and you proudly showed them how you could ride the bicycle, turn corners, and even go around in circles. Remember?

I'm thinking of your future, Jean. When you have a little seven-year-old granddaughter, will you please give me to her? I hope so. But now, please tuck me back into my Clinton's Safety Pins box-bed and cover me with my warm flannel coverlet, with the blanket stitching around the edges. I like to be warm and cozy, you know. I'm very comfortable there, and I can continue to have my happy doll-memories of the past, and my doll-dreams of the future. I'm sort of sleepy now, so goodnight and sweet dreams to you, dear Jean. Remember, Grandmother loves you very, very much. Goodnight.

Children will challenge either one's nerves or one's ideas, so it's a wise grandparent who will have an almost inexhaustible collection of ideas. Such things as a dress-up box filled with grandma's fascinating old clothing, an afternoon of baking cookies, a fingertip tour of scrapbooks and books of remembrance, a special toy box, an evening of family movies or slides, an outing to the zoo or the Santa Claus parade, and story times by the hour might suggest a few grandmotherly activities.

As children grow older, a luncheon with granddaughters might replace the toy box, or watching a grandson play football can be exchanged for the visit to the zoo. What is important is not the activity, but the relationship that is being established.

Grandma can be a great cheering squad of one as she encourages children in their schooling, musical training, scouting achievements, and similar ventures. Somehow, a word of praise from her is particularly effective.

A once-a-month family home evening with the extended family (grandparents, uncles, aunts, and cousins) has become a favorite tradition for many families who live close enough to allow this to happen. Getting together like this can bring a special closeness among family members, and it's wonderful for growing children to hear gospel lesson and testimonies from grandparents in addition to those expressed by parents. The very happiest moments for my husband and me are when all of our children are with us. Surely our joy would be even greater when another generation is added.

And no place can compare with grandmother's at Thanksgiving or Christmas time. As a grandmother, I would find much delight in planning and preparing for these occasions in order to make them crowning points of the year and highly memorable in the lives of our family members. Should circumstances prevent the family's coming to us, then if at all possible we would go to them, eager to contribute to the spirit of the day.

Through filling your life over the years with meaningful activities, many to be enjoyed with your husband and some of your time and your home shared with grandchildren, you are certain to discover new joys and fulfillment—and maybe even a few fingerprints here and there!

# 10
## To Show That It Works

*If we want to have
our homes in heaven hereafter,
we must have heaven
in our homes here.*

It's a tradition for a professor at one of our Church colleges to invite all his students to his home for an evening each semester. When asked why he puts forth the time and effort every few months to prepare an open house for several hundred students, he answered, "It's my responsibility in the classroom to teach young people about the gospel of Jesus Christ. It's my responsibility at home to show them that it works."

Such is the message of Mormonism—a remarkable blend of heavenly principles with great earthly application. Only when our homes are happy is the gospel truly working in our lives. Our Father in heaven has reserved the greatest blessings of eternity and the most sublime joys in his plan for the family.

The great goal of the gospel is to exalt families. The order of the celestial kingdom is patriarchal—a marvelous family organization will be in effect there. Our purpose in this life is to be preparing for this glorious condition and living for it now. We must ever realize that perfection is a process, not an event.

The knowledge available for accomplishing this is abundant. But it's not the just the knowing—it's the doing that counts.

In the beautiful song "I Am a Child of God" by Naomi W. Randall and Mildred T. Pettit, one line was originally written, "Teach me all that I must *know*...." That line was later changed to "Teach me all that I must *do* to live with Him some day." What a message in just one word!

I sincerely hope that you as a wife, mother, and homemaker will do the things essential for the eternal welfare of your family. May your attitudes and abilities be such that homemaking is neither beneath you nor beyond you. May you know for yourself that happiness is homemade. Then will peace and progress, joy and success be yours as a family.

It is our responsibility as parents to teach our children, through our works and example, about the gospel of Jesus Christ. It is our responsibility to show them, through our homes, that it works.

# Index